WOMEN AND HIGHER EDUCATION IN AMERICAN HISTORY

WOMEN AND HIGHER EDUCATION IN AMERICAN HISTORY

ESSAYS FROM THE
MOUNT HOLYOKE COLLEGE
SESQUICENTENNIAL SYMPOSIA

EDITED BY

JOHN MACK FARAGHER
AND FLORENCE HOWE

W·W·NORTON & COMPANY
NEW YORK   LONDON

The text of this book is composed in Electra, with
display type set in Antique Solid Roman. Composition and
manufacturing by The Maple-Vail Book Manufacturing Group.
Book design by Margaret M. Wagner.

First Edition

Library of Congress Cataloging-in-Publication Data

Women and higher education.
Bibliography: p.
Includes index.
1. Higher education of women—United States—History.
I. Faragher, John Mack, 1945–   . II. Howe, Florence.
LC1756.W663   1988   378'.08042   87–28314

ISBN 0-393-02501-2

W. W. Norton & Company, Inc., 500 Fifth Avenue, New York, N.Y. 10110
W. W. Norton & Company Ltd., 37 Great Russell Street, London WC1B 3NU

1 2 3 4 5 6 7 8 9 0

To Sarah Grimké Faragher,
now beginning her own college years

CONTENTS

v i i

Contents

v i i i

INTRODUCTION

In anticipation of the celebration of the sesquicentennial of the founding of Mount Holyoke College, scheduled for 1987, the college held a series of symposia on the history and future of women's higher education in America. The essays in this collection are selected from papers first presented at symposia held in 1983, 1984, and 1985.[1] It follows in the tradition of Mount Holyoke's celebration of anniversaries, begun in 1862, on the occasion of the twenty-fifth, when the college published a volume of student and faculty recollections of its founder, Mary Lyon. For three of the succeeding quarter-century anniversary celebrations the college issued collections of pro-

[1] Dean of Faculty Joseph J. Ellis proposed the idea for the symposia. I [John Mack Faragher] organized the first two, concentrating on the history of women's higher education; the third, focusing on the future, was organized by Joan Cocks, professor of politics. The expert services of college secretary Gwendolyn Glass and her staff made the multitude of arrangements required for the several hundred persons who attended. A lively group of scholars committed to the critical discussion of women's education supplied the intellectual exchange. Florence Howe and I worked together in the selection and editorial supervision of the essays.

grams, proceedings, and speeches, each constituting a suggestive record of views regarding this experiment in women's
education.[2]

Each of these commemorative volumes marked important
points in the history of the college. On its fiftieth anniversary
in 1887, for example, Mount Holyoke Female Seminary was
on the verge of deciding to declare itself a college, like the
other institutions of higher education for women that had been
established since the pioneer days of the 1830s. Despite this
future prospect, however, the founding struggles of the institution and the defense of the project of women's education
captured the attention of most of the speakers. Graduates and
faculty alike shared their experience of the social and cultural
opposition to anything more than the most basic primary education for women. One graduate of the 1840s told of a neigh-
boring farmer's reaction to the proposal of women's seminary
education: "If a girl can read, write and cipher as fur as the
Rule of Three 'tis all the eddication she needs." Other speakers
reviewed objections that higher learning for women was likely
to upset traditional values. The distinguished Mount Holyoke
scientist Lydia White Shattuck, for example, felt compelled to
defend her students against charges that the teaching of evolution encouraged religious skepticism. "I have yet to learn
that, because of these studies, any of our students have become
less reverent toward the Bible or less confident of the divine
love and care," she replied to critics, denying that the advanced
science curriculum of the seminary had transformed any of
her students "into agnostics or infidels."[3]

[2] Publications appeared in each of the anniversary years but 1962: *Memorial: Twenty-fifth Anniversary of the Mt. Holyoke Female Seminary* (Springfield, Mass.: S. Bowles & Co., 1862); Mrs. Sarah Locke Stowe, ed., *Semi-Centennial Celebration of Mount Holyoke Seminary, South Hadley, Mass. 1837–1887* (Springfield, Mass.: The Seminary, 1888); *The Seventy-fifth Anniversary, Mount Holyoke College* (South Hadley, Mass.: The College, 1913); *The Centenary of Mount Holyoke College, Friday and Saturday, May Seventh and Eighth, Nineteen Hundred and Thirty-Seven* (South Hadley, Mass: The College, 1937).
[3] Stowe, ed., *Semi-Centennial Celebration*: 51, 70.

But it was the worry that educated women were less likely than their uneducated sisters to marry and rear families—in short, that educated women were likely to avoid their feminine duties—that most occupied the defensive attention of speakers at these occasions. "Be not alarmed, conservative soul," one alumna assured the public in 1887, "home is, and ever will be, woman's primal kingdom." Like all the other speakers who addressed the question of women's education at the anniversary celebration, this woman held to the ideology of women's essential domesticity, which, she argued, remained uncompromised by education: "Woman is none the less queen in the home because she has taken her degree at college."

Twenty-five years later, at the anniversary celebration in 1912, another graduate took up one of the favorite conservative questions of the day: "Does the college rob the cradle?" With braggadocio she answered that "many of us have had nine children, some even more, and there are a large number of families of five and six." Yet Mount Holyoke was no exception to statistics revealing that at least a quarter of the women who graduated from college before World War I never married, double the proportion of the never-married among non graduates, and further, that while the total fertility rate of American women had fallen to fewer than four children by 1900, rates were lower still for women who delayed marriage in order to earn a college degree. The defensive sensibility, however, could not countenance these realities and tended to shut them out.[4]

Notwithstanding a certain continuity in such defensive attitudes, however, other speakers at Mount Holyoke's fiftieth anniversary testified to a conviction that the seminary was part of a veritable revolution in the lives of women. As one woman declared, "The point that most interests us and which is most pertinent to the occasion is the radical change which fifty years have wrought in the place and power of woman." Addressing

[4] Ibid.: 102; *Seventy-fifth Anniversary:* 56.

herself to what she termed the "broadening sphere of woman's life"—by which she meant the extension of women's domestic concerns to the public world through temporary careers in teaching, benevolent, and philanthropic work undertaken before marriage—she declared that "God in his providence has brought woman into personal contact with the forces that are moving the world. She has learned that her responsibilities may not be delegated to husband or sons. She has felt that inspiration that is begotten only of the consciousness that she lives in a day when her life cannot be so retired."[5]

At the jubilee celebration in 1912, alumnae and guests were entertained by a "Festival Procession," in which students, dressed in period costumes, portrayed "The Liberal Arts and Sciences." The faded photographs in the seventy-fifth anniversary volume remain delightful—college girls made up as Pythagoras and Euclid, Herodotus and John Winthrop—and reflect the importance the traditional liberal arts curriculum had assumed in the college. Speakers at the jubilee included M. Carey Thomas, president of Bryn Mawr College, and social activist Julia Lathrop, associate of Jane Addams, who some years earlier had been awarded an honorary degree by the college for her work at Hull House, women who reflected the progressive social concerns of many of the Mount Holyoke faculty and student body. Like the speakers twenty-five years earlier in 1887, these women declared their belief, albeit without the earlier references to God and family, that women's higher education was, as Thomas put it, "part and parcel of the great social revolution which is now upon us." The avowed feminist perspective of these 1912 speakers, however, marked a clear departure from the earlier sensibility. Gone was the defensive tone regarding women's education; in its place President Thomas mounted a critique of the social and cultural barriers to women's full participation in the work of the public

[5] Stowe, ed., *Semi-Centennial Celebration:* 103.

world. The great achievement of the establishment of institutions of higher education for women notwithstanding, she argued, women had "not yet won the rewards of study." Although better than half the graduates of the women's colleges took up the profession of teaching, and although women constituted a third of all graduate students preparing for careers in higher education, "even in the lower public schools," she complained, "the most responsible and highly paid positions are reserved for men, and in the few women's colleges only may women compete with men for full professorships." Male administrators, believing that women's proper sphere was in the home, failed to advance and promote their female staff.

Moreover, according to Thomas, women suffered "another and still more cruel handicap":

> They may have spent half a lifetime in fitting themselves for their chosen work and then may be asked to choose between it and marriage. No one can estimate the number of women who remain unmarried in revolt before such a horrible alternative. . . . As a result of this unsocial treatment of women there is a large and ever increasing body of celibate women. . . . When women can continue their professions and unite their incomes with their husbands' incomes men and women can afford to marry.

For its time this was a remarkable declaration. An earlier generation had argued that women's education would not subvert the patriarchial patterns of the past. For Thomas, however, the contradictions that education introduced between a woman's aspiration for meaningful public work and her needs for marriage and family posed a challenge to antiquated cultural convention and social structure. She spoke with hope and confidence of a time in the not too distant future when the "transformation of society" would have progressed to the point that women would enjoy equal opportunity "in every field of human effort including teaching and scholarship." For President Thomas, in short, home was no longer "primal." "Men do not yet understand," she declared, "that women, like themselves, find their greatest happiness in congenial work."[6]

Such a feminist perspective was even more in evidence twenty-five years later at the one hundredth anniversary celebration in 1937, held as President Mary Woolley prepared for retirement after nearly forty years at the helm and the college prepared for its first male president. Margery Corbett Ashby, president of the International Alliance of Women, warned students and alumnae against possible "delusions," fostered by women's relatively equal access to education, that the public world was similarly open. Women are graduated and begin careers, she lamented, only to find, after years of work, that "we are passed over for promotion, and that the difference between men's and women's salaries and opportunities yawns more widely. We still need the loyalty and comradeship among women that won us the world of today. We must break the vicious circle which denies us posts of leadership and responsibility." She repeated the message of other speakers at that same celebration, including Franklin Roosevelt's secretary of labor, Mount Holyoke alumna Frances Perkins: The struggle to broaden the frontiers of women's education ought now to be redirected into the struggle to expand women's social and economic opportunities in the world at large. Feminist speakers in 1937 not only dissented from the view that higher education was merely preparation for a more refined domesticity and endorsed women's aspirations for meaningful work but argued that the college must empower women for a struggle to widen opportunity in the public world.[7]

In no sense, however, did any of these feminist speakers make a case for the liberal notion of woman as merely an individual, as essentially identical with man. In company with

[6] *Seventy-fifth Anniversary:* 101–03.
[7] *Centenary of Mount Holyoke College:* 81–82, 18.

their nineteenth-century counterparts, these early-twentieth-century feminists proclaimed a belief in the importance of the differences between the sexes—differences in personality and ultimately differences in gender-based cultures. In 1912 M. Carey Thomas suggested that certain traits of character distinguished women from men: "patience, dogged persistence, unswerving pursuit of the thing itself, and a certain kind of self-sacrificing idealism." In line with her argument for extending women's public opportunities, she suggested that these feminine traits better fitted women than men for certain kinds of work, including public school teaching, nursing, and other human service careers; Thomas suggested, in fact, that women's "peculiar qualities" prepared them to be better researchers and college professors. In these comments Thomas sounded something like Reverend William S. Tyler, president of the Mount Holyoke board of trustees, who a quarter century earlier in 1887 had distinguished what he called the "individualist" or masculine side of culture from the "social" or feminine side; "manly courage and strength" on the one hand; "the intuitive ideas, the imaginative faculties, the emotional natures, the moral and religious feelings and impulses which distinguish the sex" on the other. The goal of an enlightened higher education for women, Tyler suggested, was "the equal and harmonious blending of woman's influence with that of man" and thus the cultivation of women who not only could "beautify and sanctify the home" but understood enough of men's world to "penetrate and pervade all the walks of private and social, and thus, indirectly, of public life." Thomas and Tyler may have diverged in their expectations of the educated woman's principal occupation, but they agreed in their assessment of her distinctive mentality.[8]

In her keynote address at the 1937 centenary exercises, fem-

---

[8] *Seventy-fifth Anniversary:* 102; Stowe, ed., *Semi-Centennial of Mount Holyoke College:* 124, 128.

inist historian Mary Ritter Beard offered a strong latter-day statement of a similar perspective. Cautioning against a simpleminded feminist reading of history, "which made the past all a wretched mistake," Beard stressed women's strong positive contribution to the history of human culture. We women must not forget, she argued, "the historic feminine inclination, . . . the power of intuitive insight into moral and esthetic values." As young women of the twentieth century enthusiastically entered what had hitherto been men's world—the public world of higher education and careers—there existed a grave danger, she reasoned, that they would abandon the touchstone of their own historic culture and uncritically adopt the culture of men, a culture that Beard characterized at its worst as "the secular, amoral, materialistic, mechanistic doctrine of each against all." If women had applied the male "tooth-and-claw" philosophy, she argued, "hungry mothers would have snatched the last crumb of bread from their babies, [and] feminists would have become unqualified Amazons."

Women's higher education, then, Beard argued in 1937, should seek not to obliterate but, indeed, to treasure, preserve, and extend the basic characterological and cultural differences between the genders. Beard viewed this as an especially urgent necessity in those threatening and terrifying prewar years.

> At this hour when the balance is so heavily weighted on the side of militarism and sheer force, the women who know their history and understand their role in the processes of a humane civilization can make only one decision. They must cling deliberately and firmly to their principle of history, take their stand for the cause of enlightened humanism, and make their direction of the education of girls serve the ends of that grand cause. But let there be no misunderstanding of that education. It means no mere instruction in the arts of keeping house, in child psychology, in sex wiles, in marital relations, or the technicalities of scholarship and research, however important these may be as subsidiaries. It does mean education based squarely on the feminine principle of

history, without surrender to men on the march for the kill, and
sensitive to the public responsibilities which inexorably flow from
that principle.

Loath to narrow women's cultural contribution to either refined
domesticity or professional careerism, Beard called upon women
to save men and the world men had wrought from themselves.[9]

The authors of the essays to follow examine a variety of topics.
A poignant introduction to the importance of women's education is offered by Jean Strouse's reflections on the ways in
which the *lack* of education affected three nineteenth-century
women. Linda Kerber and Joyce Antler provide broad over-
views of the higher education of American women through
the biographies of two educational pioneers who played
important roles in that history. Linda Perkins and Jeanne Noble
explore the little-known history of the college education of black
women in the nineteenth and twentieth centuries. Rosalind
Rosenberg surveys the problematic history of women in coeducational institutions. Barbara Sicherman analyzes the life and
work patterns of women graduates, while Geraldine Clifford
focuses more closely on the underappreciated profession of
teaching, the first professional career opened to American
women. In two final essays, oriented more to the future than
the past, Ann Ferguson applies contemporary feminist theory
to the prospect of higher education for women, and Ruth
Schmidt argues for the continuing importance of women's
colleges in the coming century.

These provocative essays suggest certain continuities with
the themes found in the earlier Holyoke anniversary volumes,
especially in their concern with the distinctive historical con-

[9] *Centenary of Mount Holyoke College:* 46, 55, 57, 60.

tribution of women's education, with what Ruth Schmidt calls the "verities." In Linda Kerber's essay we come to understand better the ways in which the ideology of domesticity supplied the cultural context out of which higher education for women emerged, and in the essays by Barbara Sicherman and Geraldine Clifford we see how that ideology helped shape the pattern of women's educational and career choices. Linda Perkins and Jeanne Noble demonstrate that domesticity was an important issue for black women as well. Joyce Antler and Rosalind Rosenberg suggest the ways in which higher education failed to meet women's special needs. Echoing both the vision and the passion of Mary Beard, Ann Ferguson argues for a sophisticated model of woman's distinctive "moral voice."

Perhaps the most obvious departure reflected in this volume, as compared with the earlier ones, is the dramatic development of women's history itself. In her Mount Holyoke address, as elsewhere, Mary Beard called upon women to "know their history," and in a remarkable outpouring of feminist scholarship that has been tied directly to the revitalization of the women's movement over the past two decades, historians responding to that challenge have achieved impressive new understandings. Most of these essays are part and parcel of this historical renaissance. They may be read as "needs and opportunities" reports on the state of contemporary scholarship on the history of women's higher education; indeed, one of our hopes for this anniversary collection is that it will in some measure stimulate further consideration of the important issues raised herein. "Woman *is* and *makes* history," Beard declared in 1937; in 1987 that is equally true.

JOHN MACK FARAGHER

WOMEN AND HIGHER EDUCATION
IN AMERICAN HISTORY

JEAN STROUSE
Private Strife: Some Social Consequences of the Anatomical Distinction Between the Sexes

To highlight some questions about women and education, I am going to describe three young women growing up in the nineteenth century: Elizabeth Barrett, Alice James, and Maggie Tulliver, the central figure in George Eliot's novel *The Mill on the Floss*. I take the liberty of mixing real life and fiction since although George Eliot did not write in autobiographical terms about the issues I am going to discuss, she illuminated them brilliantly in this novel, which came, more directly than any of her other books, out of her own experience. The primary conflicts in each of these three lives, separated as the young girls were by time and nationality, had to do with femininity, education, and the strictures imposed by family and society on the condition of being female.

In celebrating the 150th anniversary of the founding of Mount

JEAN STROUSE *is a writer and biographer who lives in New York City.* Copyright © 1987 *by Jean Strouse. Reprinted by permission of the author.*

Holyoke College and Mary Lyon's then-revolutionary notion that women needed higher education to become full participants in the worlds they inhabited, it seems particularly useful to see how powerfully the *lack* of education affected these three extraordinary lives—how intensely preoccupied each woman was with her inadequate preparation for intellectual life and how deeply this lack affected her whole sense of self and capability. For of course, the psychological and the social are not at all separate spheres: If early-nineteenth-century society assumed women were not worth educating, that assumption profoundly influenced most women's attitudes toward themselves and severely limited the range of paths they might imagine taking. Mary Lyon was an exception, and she created an institution that helped move all of American society toward making what was then exceptional—the education of women— into a norm. Elizabeth Barrett and George Eliot were exceptions as well; in spite of scant formal education, they managed to get what intellectual training they needed by unconventional means and to create lasting—in Eliot's case, truly great— literary work. Alice James belongs in a category of her own— she was what the James family would have called "an interesting failure"—and her career of neurasthenic invalidism was in a sad way her solution to the problem of being intellectually ambitious, inadequately educated, and female.

Elizabeth Barrett, born in England in 1806, was a tiny child with great strength of character. She wrote in an early autobiography: "I was always of a determined, if thwarted violent disposition. . . . My actions and temper were infinitely more inflexible at three years old than now at fourteen." She speaks of having "reigned" alone in the nursery—but not for long. A first son, Edward, was born into the Barrett household when Elizabeth was two, and the boy was greeted by Mr. Barrett as the "crown of his house." When Edward was about a year old and beginning, under adoring parental eyes, to walk, Elizabeth first displayed what she later termed the "excessive passion" of the dispossessed. As Edward grew into active boyhood, his masculine prerogatives aroused in her a fierce "spirit of emulation," and she felt increasingly "inconsolable for not being born a man."

Elizabeth Barrett soon became a rebellious tomboy—in her own words, "much more wild and much more mad" than her sisters or brother. She hated petticoats and sewing, loved climbing trees, ladders, and walls. She refused to study with the governess who had been hired to teach her sisters. Edward had a tutor, who taught him Greek and Latin, and Elizabeth, repudiating what she called the "subserviency of opinion which is generally considered necessary to feminine softness," insisted on sharing in Edward's lessons. She became quite a little scholar, all the while feeling "a steady indignation against nature who made me a woman, and a determinate resolution to dress up in men's clothes as soon as ever I was free of the nursery, and go into the world 'to seek my fortune.' " It was Edward, however, who went out into the world, leaving his envious sister and the enclosed world of their country manor (named, appropriately enough, Hope End) for London and public school. He was twelve when he left; Elizabeth, fourteen. She had, until then, been able to siphon an education off her brother's, coaxing her way into intellectual comradeship, charting a solitary path toward the emancipation she had read about, when she was twelve, in Mary Wollstonecraft's *A Vindication of the Rights of Women*. Now, as Edward drove out through the lodge gates at Hope End, Elizabeth wrote: "The Dream has faded—it is over."

For a year she struggled rather successfully against her consequent rage and rebellion. She wrote that her character was "still as proud, as wilful, as impatient of controul, as impetuous, but Thanks be to God it is restrained." To her friends she seemed to have "undergone a revolution," she continued, "but to myself it is well known that the same violent inclinations are in my inmost heart and that altho' habitual restraint has become almost a part of myself yet were I once to lose the rigid rein I might again be hurled with Phaeton far from everything human . . . everything reasonable!" When the time came for Edward to leave again for his second year at school, Elizabeth lost that rigid rein, taking to her bed in "prolonged and spectacular paroxysms of pain." Exactly what went on in this breakdown is not clear. One acute and sympathetic doctor observed that her "mind has ceased in a great degree to engage in those investigations and pursuits which formerly constituted its greatest delight." Elizabeth took full advantage of what we would now call the "secondary gains" of her illness, staying in bed with her parents hovering anxiously nearby, while her sisters tended to the domestic chores and called her the "most useless person in the house."

Elizabeth Barrett turned her "violent inclinations" in on her own mind and body and continued to adore her brother, Edward, enshrining him in an image of ideal virtue. When he drowned in a sailing accident in 1840, she broke down completely and later told a friend that she had only narrowly escaped "absolute hopeless madness." During this acute breakdown she could not read or understand what people said: "The mind seemed to myself broken up into fragments." Gradually she came back from this edge of madness, but years later she wrote, "The griefs that are incurable are those which have our own sins festering in them." If she had any further inkling of hatred or murderous feelings toward Edward, she never acknowledged it; instead, she blamed "nature who made me a woman" and her impetuous, violent character. She stayed in her sickroom, writing poetry, convinced of the ineradicable evil of her nature, attended by her stern but adoring father, until she was forty years old, when Robert Browning came along to lure her slowly back to life. Browning, who worked patiently at her "cure" for long, difficult years (and for his own, intricately complex reasons), wrote at one point a line that might well be inscribed over the doorways of all psychologists' offices. "Of all fighting," Browning observed, "the warfare with shadows— what a work is *there.*"

George Eliot intended originally to call the novel that became *The Mill on the Floss* "Sister Maggie," and for all its other themes, it is at heart the story of a brother and sister, Tom and Maggie Tulliver. They live with their parents in the provincial English town of St. Ogg's. Tom, a few years older than Maggie, knows his place in their small world, and believes with serene confidence in his own uncompromising sense of right and wrong. Maggie, by contrast, is wild, rebellious, always in some kind of trouble; she's constantly tossing her masses of unruly dark hair out of her eyes and struggling to subdue her tempestuous energy. She is clever, active, insatiably curious— and those are not the qualities good little St. Ogg's girls are made of. Yet Maggie wants, above all, to be good and to be loved, especially by her father and Tom. She was, writes Eliot, "rather in awe of Tom's superiority, for he was the only person who called her knowledge 'stuff,' and did not feel surprised at her cleverness. Tom, indeed, was of opinion that Maggie was a silly little thing; all girls were silly—they couldn't throw a stone so as to hit anything, couldn't do anything with a pocketknife, and were frightened at frogs. Still he was very fond of his sister, and meant always to take care of her, make her his housekeeper, and punish her when she did wrong."

Tom, like Edward Barrett, goes off to school, to study with the Reverend Walter Stelling, though Tom would much rather study guns and horses than Latin and Euclid. Maggie, who loves reading and learning, comes to visit him at the Stellings', and soon she and Tom are arguing about whether or not she couldn't do schoolwork, too. Later that day she appeals to Mr.

Stelling. " '[C]ouldn't I do Euclid,' " she asks, " 'and all Tom's lessons, if you were to teach me instead of him?' "

" 'No, you couldn't,' said Tom, indignantly. 'Girls can't do Euclid: can they, sir?'

" 'They can pick up a little of everything, I daresay,' said Mr. Stelling. 'They've a great deal of superficial cleverness, but they couldn't go far into anything. They're quick and shallow.' "

Eliot goes on:

> Tom, delighted with this verdict, telegraphed his triumph by wagging his head at Maggie behind Mr. Stelling's chair. As for Maggie, she had hardly ever been so mortified. She had been so proud to be called "quick" all her little life, and now it appeared that this quickness was the brand of inferiority. It would have been better to be slow, like Tom.
>
> "Ha, ha! Miss Maggie!" said Tom, when they were alone, "you see it's not such a fine thing to be quick. You'll never go far into anything, you know."
>
> And Maggie was so oppressed by this dreadful destiny that she had no spirit for a retort.

George Eliot made her own late escape from this "dreadful destiny" through ideas, writing, a masculine pseudonym (her real name was Mary Ann Evans), and the disciplined use of her mind, but her acute sense of just what she'd escaped comes through in melodramatic paragraphs on Maggie's deprivation. Eliot writes:

> [Maggie's life struggles had] lain almost entirely within her own soul, one shadowy army fighting another, and the slain shadows forever rising again, [while Tom] was engaged in a dustier, noisier warfare, grappling with more substantial obstacles, and gaining more definite conquests. So it has been since the days of Hecuba, and of Hector, tamer of horses: inside the gates, the women with streaming hair and uplifted hands offering prayers, watching the world's combat from afar, filling their long, empty days with

8

memories and fears; outside, the men, in fierce struggle with things divine and human, quenching memory in the stronger light of purpose, losing the sense of dread and even of wounds in the hurrying ardor of action.

And elsewhere:

[Maggie] was as lonely in her trouble as if she had been the only girl in the civilized world of that day who had come out of her school-life with a soul untrained for inevitable struggles—with no other part of her inherited share in the hard-won treasures of thought, which generations of painful toil have laid up for the race of men, than shreds and patches of feeble literature and false history—with much futile information about Saxon and other kings of doubtful example—but unhappily quite without that knowledge of the irreversible laws within and without her, which, governing the habits, becomes morality, and developing the feelings of submission and dependence, becomes religion—as lonely in her trouble as if every other girl besides herself had been cherished and watched over by elder minds not forgetful of their own early time when need was keen and impulse strong.

As is clear from these passages, Eliot mourns for Maggie not simply a lack of book learning, but the absence of wide knowledge about human experience itself, that "training" of the soul that has found cohesive expression in morality and religion. Maggie's radical innocence becomes her doom. To summarize the rest of the story much too briefly, Maggie fights to subdue her active, energetic nature, to conform to the St. Ogg's ideal of passive, submissive, pure feminine virtue. She has no moral code of her own to supplant society's hollow standards; her only guide, and desperate need, is the love and approval of others. Her cousin Lucy Deane *does* manage to embody that feminine ideal—and to gain the conventional rewards: Tom Tulliver loves Lucy, but Lucy becomes secretly engaged to another man, Stephen Guest. Then Maggie, against all propriety and reason, falls in love with Stephen, and here her innocence takes its tragic turn, for though she tries desperately to resist these "illicit" impulses, the draw of sexuality and her need to be loved prove much stronger than social sanctions. Maggie goes out in a boat to talk with Stephen, and they are—both literally and symbolically—swept away by the strong current and carried so far downriver that they have to spend the night away from St Ogg's. Stephen wants her to marry him, and she languidly submits to a moment of present happiness. Though Eliot's language here is sexual, she is talking about emotions rather than actions. In the morning—after an innocent night—Maggie's conscience awakens, and horrified at her own weakness, she returns to St. Ogg's. There, of course, she must face the consequences of her apparent transgression—and the worst punishment comes from Tom, "trembling and white with disgust and indignation," who tells her, "You will find no home with me. . . . You have disgraced us all. . . . I wash my hands of you forever. You don't belong to me."

When Eliot wrote this book, in 1859 and 1860, she was living with the essayist and biographer George Henry Lewes, to whom she was not married, and her own brother, Isaac, had closed *his* door on his "disgraceful" sister. In a recent essay Cynthia Ozick observed that the secret in Eliot's life "is the dense burden of humiliation imposed by an adored brother more cruel and rigid than society itself." In Maggie and Tom, however, Eliot finds a resolution that is at once revenge and self-punishment and the restoration of lost love. A cataclysmic flood brings the book to its close. Tom, who has never forgiven Maggie, is trapped in his house, and Maggie fights the storm and raging currents alone in a small boat to come rescue him. She succeeds, but their boat is then crushed by a huge fragment of floating machinery, and the novel ends with these words: "The boat reappeared—but brother and sister had gone down in an embrace never to be parted: living through again in one supreme moment, the days when they had clasped their little hands in love, and roamed the daisied fields together."

The Mill on the Floss was published in 1860. Alice James, born in America in 1848, read it in late adolescence and declared it her favorite book. It is not difficult to see why. Alice was the only girl—and the youngest—in a family of five. Her eldest two brothers were, of course, William and Henry James, and Henry, who probably understood his sister better than anyone else ever did, observed years later: "In our family group, girls seem scarcely to have had a chance." Like Elizabeth Barrett and Maggie Tulliver, Alice had an early period of prelapsarian parity with another brother, Rob, in the nursery. Though Rob teased and mildly tortured the little girl who had displaced him as the favored youngest, the two did play and roughhouse together in what was probably the freest heterosexual physical contact of Alice's life. All too soon, Rob left their small shared world to go out and play with the big boys. Alice stayed behind— at first because she was the youngest and then, apparently forever, because she was a girl.

When the James children were young, their highly eccentric and independently wealthy father, Henry, Sr., devoted himself to what he called their "sensuous education," exposing them to books, theater, music, and art, searching out unusual schools for the boys in Europe and America, then quickly finding those schools disappointing and dragging the entire family off to a new city or continent in search of the perfect education that existed only in his mind. For all his originality on the subject of education, James, Sr., did not believe in the education of women. He thought his boys would learn to be "good"—to struggle against selfishness and the evils inherent in the universe—through wide intellectual experience and the interesting uses of perception. Girls, on the other hand, he held to be good by nature; they could dispense with interesting ideas.

In 1853 James, Sr., published an article in *Putnam's Monthly* magazine on "Woman and the 'Woman's Movement.'" He wrote:

The very virtue of woman, her practical sense, which leaves her indifferent to past and future alike, and keeps her the busy blessing of the present hour, disqualifies her for all didactic dignity. Learning and wisdom do not become her. Even the ten commandments seem unamiable and superfluous on her lips, so much should her own pure pleasure form the best outward law for man. We say to her, "Do not tell me, beautiful doctor, I pray you, what one ought or ought not to do; any musty old professor in the next college is quite competent to that: tell me only what I shall do to please you, and it shall be done, though the heavens fall!"

In spite of his opposition to female intellect, however, James, Sr., delighted in the quickness of his daughter's mind. He encouraged her to read, and they spent long hours alone together in his study, talking, joking, trading opinions and insults. Her early education, then, was a haphazard mix of encouragement and slight; her father enjoyed sharing knowledge with her piecemeal, but more as a pleasant way to amuse himself than as a serious effort to train her mind. Ambiguity characterized Alice's lifelong estimates of the female sex and of her own mental prowess; toward the end of her life she wondered, wryly, whether "if I had had any education, I should be more, or less, of a fool than I am." She then went on to contradict by example that assertion of foolishness, for the modesty, wit, and irony of her remarks present a clear contrast to her father's solemn, inflated rhetoric on the subject of female "didactic dignity": Education, she wrote, "would have deprived me surely of those exquisite moments of mental flatulence which every now and then inflate the cerebral vacuum with a delicious sense of latent possibilities—of stretching oneself to cosmic limits, and who would ever give up the reality of dreams for relative knowledge?"

Alice's eldest brother, William, constantly lavished on her his extravagant affection. He was profoundly preoccupied with his own psychological troubles, however, and from very early on there is a distinctly sexual tone to his teasing. One night in

1859, when he was seventeen and Alice eleven, William composed a "sonnate" in her honor, and invited the family into the parlor to hear him sing it:

> The moon was mildly beaming
> Upon the summer sea
> I lay entranced and dreaming
> My Alice sweet, of thee.
> Upon the seashore lying
> Upon the yellow sand
> The foaming waves replying
> I vowed to ask thy hand.
>
> I swore to ask thy hand, my love
> I vowed to ask thy hand.
> I wished to join myself to thee
> By matrimonial band.
>
> So very proud, but yet so fair
> The look you on me threw
> You told me I must never dare
> To hope for love from you.
>
> Your childlike form, your golden hair
> I never more may see
> But goaded on by dire despair
> I'll drown within the sea.
>
> Adieu to love! Adieu to life!
> Since I may not have thee,
> My Alice sweet, to be my wife,
> I'll drown me in the sea!
> I'll drown me in the sea, my love
> I'll drown—me in—the sea.

"Alice took it very coolly," William reported by mail the next day to his father, who was away in London, and another brother, Wilky, wrote that the song "excited a good deal of laughter among the audience assembled." Alice learned to share in the family amusement at this sort of carrying-on, watching herself as object and managing to detach herself from the flushed confusions involved in also being the subject of this incest-uous diversion.

As the only female James child she grew up like a fragile tropical plant, fed on special preparations of solicitude, curi-osity, and indifference. At around age twelve she began to have difficulty with her "delicate" temperament, and by nineteen she was having full-fledged nervous breakdowns. She was diagnosed as neurasthenic, hysterical, and rheumatoid; the pains moved from her head to her legs to her stomach to her chest; she tried rest cures, exercise, hot baths, cold baths, galvanic currents, and finally—as she was dying—hypnosis. She became, in effect, a professional invalid, and no writing career or Rob-ert Browning was able to rescue her from these incapacitating illnesses. She wrote, toward the end of her life, a passage in her diary that described her first acute nervous breakdown, at the age of nineteen; this extraordinary account highlights, in vivid, pre-Freudian language, the kinds of conflicts we have also seen in Elizabeth Barrett and Maggie Tulliver.

Alice had been reading, in 1890, an essay by William called "The Hidden Self," in which he discussed Pierre Janet's work with hysterical patients in France and the "contractions of the field of consciousness" the French philosopher had observed in the hysteric mind. One part of the body or mind splits off from normal consciousness, reported William, and is virtually abandoned; an entire leg, for instance, becomes anesthetized, and loses not only all sensation but all memory of past sensa-tion as well. In her diary Alice praised William's mapping of this psychological terrain and then turned to survey the history of her own illness, in particular the hysterical "abandoning" of that crucial organ her brain. Both the episodes she recounts here took place when she was trying to do intellectual work— to participate in the realm to which her father and two eldest brothers had staked such definitive claim.

She wrote:

I have passed thro' an infinite succession of conscious abandonments, and in looking back now I see how it began in my childhood, altho' I wasn't conscious of the necessity until . . . I broke down first, acutely, and had violent turns of hysteria. As I lay prostrate after the storm with my mind luminous and active and susceptible of the clearest, strongest impressions, I saw so distinctly that it was a fight simply between my body and my will, a battle in which the former was to be triumphant to the end. Owing to some physical weakness, excess of nervous susceptibility, the moral power pauses, as it were for a moment, and refuses to maintain muscular sanity, worn out with the strain of its constabulary functions. As I used to sit immovable reading in the library with waves of violent inclination [that is the exact phrase Elizabeth Barrett used] suddenly invading my muscles taking some one of their myriad forms such as throwing myself out of the window, or knocking off the head of the benignant pater as he sat with his silver locks, writing at his table, it used to seem to me that the only difference between me and the insane was that I had not only all the horrors and suffering of insanity but the duties of doctor, nurse, and straitjacket imposed upon me, too. . . . When the fancy took me of a morning at school to study my lessons instead of shirking or wiggling thro' the most impossible sensations of upheaval, violent revolt in my head overtook me so that I had to "abandon" my brain, as it were. So it has always been, anything that sticks of itself is free to do so, but conscious and continuous cerebration is an impossible exercise and from just behind the eyes my head feels like a dense jungle into which no ray of light has ever penetrated.

In other words, Alice's conflicts required her to give up the attempt to use her mind in any serious way. "Mind," in her family, was an attribute of masculinity, and though she desperately wanted some intellectual ground of her own to stand on, she couldn't risk entering the lists in competition with those powerful brothers, couldn't relinquish her desperate need for love and approval, couldn't reject and couldn't accept her father's notions of feminine virtue. And so she spent her best energies in the illness that rendered her literally in-valid.

Certain similarities in these three accounts are quite striking. All three girls were passionately envious of the educational prerogatives of their brothers and bitterly disappointed when the process of growing up lighted the divergent paths to be followed by males and females. All three tried earnestly to conform to their families' and societies' standards of feminine comportment and virtue, and all three rebelled violently against these standards—Eliot the most successfully, although she suffered all her life with ill health and incapacitating depressions. Elizabeth Barrett and Alice James split their "bad" rages and frustrations off into illnesses that seemed to attack them; these mysterious maladies caricatured the ambiguous ideal of female helplessness and quite specifically deprived both women of the ability to do intellectual work. Elizabeth, at her worst, could not read or understand spoken words; her mind "seemed . . . broken up into fragments." Alice, at *her* worst, found "conscious and continuous cerebration an impossible exercise," and her head felt "like a dense jungle into which no ray of light has ever penetrated."

Sigmund Freud's famous 1925 essay on women, "Some Psychological Consequences of the Anatomical Distinction Between the Sexes," focuses on little girls' envy of boys' biological endowments and traces the "consequences" of this anatomical difference in the psychological lives of women. Clearly, in the three stories I've just told, there is intense envy of maleness, as each of these girls perceives what her brother has and what she lacks. Elizabeth Barrett resolved to dress up in men's clothes and go into the world to seek her fortune; George Eliot took a man's name; Alice James referred repeatedly to her "miserable" and "disgusting" sex, and when her brother Rob had his first son, she congratulated him on the "noble sex of the creature." Yet it was not just biology that so radically separated these three from their brothers; anatomical facts symbolized the difference, but it was—still is—the social and psychological *responses* to biology that determine the real shape and content of life. The prerogatives of masculinity—access to education, freedom to go out into the world, the training and self-confidence to engage with "things divine and human," in George Eliot's words, to share in the "hard-won treasures of thought which generations of painful toil have laid up for the race of man"—those were the privileges these three girls envied with such consuming passion.

Looking at these lives now makes clear how dramatically the psychological and social consequences of sex differences have changed in the course of the past century, yet I don't think we're so far removed from that time and those conflicts that we can't hear their echoes in our own lives. Perhaps the single most effective and far-reaching change has been the slow process begun by pioneers such as Mary Lyon—of gaining for women that share in the hard-won treasures of thought so sorely missed by Elizabeth Barrett, George Eliot, and Alice James.

LINDA K. KERBER
"Why Should Girls Be Learn'd and Wise?": Two Centuries of Higher Education for Women as Seen Through the Unfinished Work of Alice Mary Baldwin

Alice Mary Baldwin was a formidable American educator; a historian, who received her Ph.D. from the University of Chicago, she is best known as the author of a long-standard monograph on New England ministers in the era of the American Revolution. She spent her career as dean of the women's college of what is now Duke University. Overworked and underpaid, she had trouble fitting research projects into her day and published little after her doctoral dissertation.

Baldwin's life and work are exemplary of the issues and major patterns that I see in the history of higher education for women from the mid-eighteenth to the late nineteenth century. First, in the course of her career she was forced to reflect on the situation of women's colleges; at the end of her life this

LINDA K. KERBER *is May Brodbeck Professor in the Liberal Arts at the University of Iowa, Iowa City, Iowa.*

restrained, discreet, woman set on paper her own bitter criticism of the way Duke University had treated its women's college and its dean. She ordered this account sealed for twenty years; it has only recently been opened. Thus her voice contributes to our understanding of the issues of higher education for women in the first half of the twentieth century. Second, in the fraction of her time that she could devote to research in early American history, she found herself increasingly drawn to the study of women's experience. Through her notes and drafts of essays we watch a fine mind struggling to write women's history without the matrix of support on which we can now rely. In 1938 she could not demand attention for her narrative of two colonial sisters who hungered for more intellectual challenge than their community could provide except by offering them as "quaint." By the time she died, in 1961, she was no longer treating women's experience apologetically. Left unfinished among her papers were notes and drafts for an essay tentatively called "The Reading of Women in the Colonies before 1750." She now set herself to defend colonial women from the charge that they "ordinarily read very little" and that "intellectual attainments were not expected of the weaker sex."

I do not know whether Baldwin realized that her own career and the research on which she was embarked were parts of the same large story; that she was in effect a character in the next to last act of a play which had featured her heroine, the eighteenth-century Bostonian Jane Colman Terrell, in its first act. For all its complexity the history of higher education for women in America has been at base a single story: the account of a continuing quest by determined women for access to books and instruction, always resisting the assumption, as much a part of our legacy from the Greeks and Romans as is the architecture of the Parthenon, that women's minds are naturally suited merely to the trivial. Before we can begin to search for *institutions* of higher education for women in America, we must first watch individual women struggling to clear a space for their own intellectual activity, struggling to defend themselves against the charge that intellectual effect was inappropriate, even dangerous, when attempted by a woman.[1]

We may discern three distinct periods or stages in the history of higher education for women in the eighteenth and nineteenth centuries. The first begins in 1700 and extends to 1775. These dates are merely symbolic; the situation of 1700 could be found in the late seventeenth century as well. In those years female literacy grew, but there were no institutions of higher education for females. Women who aspired to an education more complex than the three Rs had to find their own mentors in a culture which was highly skeptical of their efforts.

The second period extends from independence in 1776 to 1833; we might label it the "Era of the Great Debate over the Capacities of Women's Minds." Again 1776 is symbolic, while 1833 marks the opening of Oberlin College and the extension of collegiate opportunity to women. Continuing improvement in female literacy, a political revolution which articulated the need for the education of succeeding generations of moral citizens, and the assertion by some articulate women of their need for institutional support resulted in the questioning of inherited assumptions about the incapacity of women for higher education and in the establishment of schools for girls with serious aspirations. Ultimately the first women were welcomed at Oberlin.

The third period of about fifty years opens with Oberlin's founding and ends in the 1880s; 1875 marked the founding of Wellesley and Smith, 1885 the opening of Bryn Mawr, 1889 Barnard. This was a period characterized by increasing accessibility to women of institutions of higher education—some

[1] All references to Baldwin's work are based on the Alice Mary Baldwin papers in the Duke University Archives, especially the typescript "Two Sisters of Old Boston," c. 1938, and her miscellaneous notes, on cards and on sheets of paper, filed as "The Reading of Women," c. 1961.

coeducational, as in state universities like those of Iowa and Missouri; others dedicated to women alone. In 1775 there was not a single institution of higher education which included women among its students; a century later there were dozens which a woman might enter. Not many by today's standards, certainly, but an extraordinary contrast with a century before.

Through all these years, however, there hummed, like the steady continuo of the harpsichord, the constant complaint of the skeptic, versified by John Trumbull at the end of the eighteenth century:

> Why should girls be learn'd and wise?
> Books only serve to spoil their eyes.
> The studious eye but faintly twinkles
> And reading paves the way to wrinkles.

In the late 1930s Alice Baldwin wrote a narrative which she called "Two Sisters of Old Boston." It serves well as an introduction to our first era in the history of higher education for women. Although Baldwin did not explicitly mark the careers of the Colman sisters as emblems of the fate of the colonial women who hungered for advanced education, that implication is embedded in her account. This summary of the story draws on Baldwin's draft and on her 1961 notes.

Jane and Abigail were the daughters of Benjamin Colman, A.B., Harvard, 1692, minister of the Brattle Street Church in Boston. Jane, the elder, was born in 1702. The girls read the poems of Elizabeth Singer Rowe, of Pope, Blackmore, and Waller. Jane probably was familiar with some of the Latin poets as well, since later she wrote a poem in imitation of Horace. Jane's poems testified to her hunger for learning:

> Come now, fair Muse, and fill my empty mind,
> With rich ideas, great and unconfin'd . . .

O let me burn with *Sappho's* noble Fire,
But not like her for faithless man expire.

Benjamin Colman respected Jane's quest for "great and unconfin'd" ideas; in 1725 he admitted that "with the Advantages of my liberal Education at School & College, I have no reason to think but that your genius in writing would have excelled mine." At the same time, however, he warned her that writing poetry was indulgent; she should spend her time in reading and in devotion.

But Jane Colman was unlucky in her husband. Ebenezer Terrell was a minister at Medford; Baldwin assessed him as a smart but humorless man. Of his wife, the historian wrote, he "was surprised, so he said, to find her so accomplished. He thought she needed a more solid diet, so he read to her in the evenings 'Divinity, History, Physick, Controversy. . . .' "

"The story," wrote Baldwin, "told in the old letters and in the phrasing of the day, makes very clear the demands upon her young body and the conflicts of her mind and spirit." By the time Jane was twenty years old she had come to be fearful for her salvation and to regret her reading of fiction. Jane Colman Terrell died at the age of twenty-seven; at her death her father's colleague the Reverend John Adams thought to honor her by a poem which praised her writing, accepting it because Jane Terrell was

Free from ambition . . .
Nor was she vain, nor stain'd with those Neglects,
In which too learned Females lose their Sex—

The story of the younger sister, Abigail, is more tormented. "Nabby," as she was called, was twelve when Jane gave up romances; Jane urged: "[L]et me beg of you not to spend any part of your precious time in reading *Romances* and idle *Poems*, which tend only to raise false ideas and impure Images in the

Mind, and leave a vile Tincture upon it." Abigail nevertheless "gave herself to Reading from her Childhood," reported her father, "and soon to writing. She wanted not a Taste for what was excellent in Books, more especially of a Poetical Turn or Relish. . . . Thus run her too soon and too far into the reading of Novels, &c., for which God in his righteous Providence afterwards punished her by suffering her to leave her Father's House, to the Grief of her Friends and the Surprise of the Town."

Colman assumed a clear connection between Nabby's reading and her elopement with the young rake Alfred Dennie, who took her to New Hampshire, where they were married by, horrors, "a Priest of the Church of England." The rest of the tale is tragic. Their wedding night was interrupted by a constable sent by Colman to bring them back to Boston until their marriage could be proved legal. There were desperate fights over Nabby's inheritance and Dennie's expenditure of her money. Nabby claimed that she loved Dennie "with a Love stronger than Death," her father sighed that "Circumstances call for Humiliation, shame, and mourning," and a family friend accused Dennie of giving his wife "a foul disease." Shortly before she died, Abigail sighed that "I ought to be the subject of a Tragedy as noble as that of Cato's."

Stories like Abigail's would be told and retold for at least another century as a way of warning young girls to avoid misalliance; the theme has less to do with our subject of higher education and more to do with the eighteenth-century version of the Harlequin romance.[2] But what is significant for our purposes is that both sisters became emblems of caution against reading. Abigail's reading was thought to have drawn her into irresponsible behavior. Jane managed to maintain her intellectual interests without discrediting her character, but it seemed, as Reverend Adams put it, a near thing. In 1961 Baldwin

[2] See, for example, Hannah Webster Foster, *The Coquette* (1979).

decided to find out how typical the Colman girls had been. She suspected that the worry about novel reading had been overstated and not only for poor Nabby: "In the wills and inventories which I have been able to find [in New York] there is no mention of any novel or romance." In fact, there were few novels or romances in the colonies before 1750. "Usually authors have been contented to say that for the most part women were interested in household affairs, in embroidery, painting, perhaps a smattering of French. . . ." Baldwin was skeptical; she also suspected that these authors were repeating each other. She embarked on a search of wills, of printed library lists and diaries. She found women reading *The Spectator*, Shakespeare, Burton's *Anatomy of Melancholy*, Addison, Price, Congreve, Pope, Dryden. Baldwin died before she could finish this essay. But she had clearly established that the range of women's reading was far wider than her contemporaries had thought. Among her notes was a charming tale of a woman who supervised the studies of her descendants even after death: "One morning in 1780 Mrs. Latham said she was reading *The Turkish Spy* when she saw a specter of an elderly woman. One of the family said that his mother had been sent to reprove her for reading a novel on the Sabbath Day. The ghost lady was Mrs. Mary Smith who was born in 1697 and had willed all her books to be equally divided among her three sons and three granddaughters."

Baldwin's successors, among whom I count myself, have confirmed her suggestions: first, that eighteenth-century women's reading was not confined to fiction; second, that women faced severe criticism when they ventured away from household matters. Even this hesitant quest for higher learning was constrained by factors of race and class: inaccessible to the poor and to black women, attempted only by the most undaunted of the white upper middle class and the most sheltered of the wealthy.

In *The Wealth of Nations*, published just at the end of this period, Adam Smith sensitively noticed that there were few institutions in England dedicated to the education of women. He suggested that this was because women were not thought to need an education that would draw them outside the home into a world of commerce, politics, and the unpredictable. Boys, in contrast, required an education that gave them the skills needed to respond to the public world. Smith wrote: "There is nothing useless or absurd or fantastical in the common course of women's education. They can be taught what their parents or guardians judge necessary or useful for them to learn. They are taught nothing else."[3] Since parents, in effect, can predict what a woman is going to need to know, she can be trained at home to face that life. It was not anticipated that women would encounter the uncertain and the unexpected, "the absurd or the fantastical." The girl who, like Jane Colman, hungered for more than she "needed" was incomprehensible to her contemporaries. Modern social historians have counseled us to look at change over the *durée longue*, the long term. Beneath a veneer of stability major changes were under way throughout the eighteenth century, and they would come with breathtaking speed at the end. Like the bourgeoisie of the traditional Western civilization course, literacy was slowly rising through the early modern period. Literacy did not increase at the same rate for each class, nor was it displayed to an equal degree by each sex within each class, but during the first half century of the Republic's history what might be called a "literacy gap" between men and women was closing in the northern states. Studying deed signing in Windsor, Connecticut, Linda Auwers finds that nine out of ten of the wealthiest 90 percent of women who were born in the 1740s were able to sign their name on deeds—a marked improvement not only over contemporary England but also over the America of a hundred years before,

---

[3] Adam Smith, *An Inquiry into the Nature and Causes of the Wealth of Nations*, ed. Edwin Canaan (New York: Modern Library 1937): bk. V, ch. 1, pt. iii, part 2, 734.

when only 40 percent could sign.[4] Studying towns in the upper Connecticut River valley for the years of the early Republic, William Gilmore reports nearly universal literacy for men of all classes by the 1780s and 80 percent female literacy for the richest eight-tenths of the population.[5]

These figures cannot be generalized to all America. They are specific to region; the South lagged far behind, and as late as 1850 one out of five white women in the South continued illiterate.[6] They are specific to race; literacy was much lower among free blacks because they lacked both opportunity and institutional support, and of course, literacy was intentionally stifled among slaves. They are also specific to class; reliance on evidence from deeds means we are learning only about people who had property of which to dispose. Even so, these figures are extraordinary. They perhaps can be explained by the observation that the two major pressures encouraging literacy—the Reformation and the Commercial Revolution—found less opposition in New England than in Europe. Virtually all denominations encouraged reading by believers, and even rural farms were tied to a commercial trading network. It is beginning to seem that in the years of the early Republic New England women were the most literate women in Western society. Skills once regarded as those of the powerful— reading and writing—were distributed among American women to an unprecedented extent.

Moreover, the generations of women who lived through the American Revolution and the first years of the early Republic were aware—to varying degrees—that they were living through

[4] Linda Auwers, "Reading the Marks of the Past: Exploring Female Literacy in Colonial Windsor, Connecticut," *Historical Methods*, XIII (1980): 204–214.

[5] William Gilmore, "Elementary Literacy on the Eve of the Industrial Revolution: Trends in Rural New England, 1760–1830," *Proceedings of the American Antiquarian Society* 92 (1982): 114–26.

[6] Maris Vinovskis and Richard Bernard, "Beyond Catharine Beecher: Female Education in the Antebellum Period," *Signs* 3 (1978): 856–69.

a strategic moment in the history of the female intellect. Believing as they did that republics rested on the virtue of their citizens, revolutionary leaders needed to believe that Americans of subsequent generations would continue to display the moral character that a republic required. The role of guarantor of civic virtue, however, could not be assigned to a particular branch of government. Instead it was hoped that other agencies—churches, schools, families—would fulfill that function. Within families, the crucial role was thought to be the mother's, a role combining political and educational obligation which I have called the "Republican Mother."[7]

Contemporaries could not help noticing the change, just as we do, reading women's correspondence. Benjamin Franklin, for example, received occasional hesitant and almost illiterate notes from his wife, Deborah, and his friend Margaret Stevenson, his landlady in London—that is, from his female contemporaries—but he received fluent letters from his Sarah and from Stevenson's daughter Polly. Both these younger women benefited from the improvements in women's elementary education which occurred in the late eighteenth century. Formal facilities for teaching girls multiplied. Quakers established coeducational schools. Moravians established pairs of schools for boys and girls. New England schools began to hold summer sessions for girls and younger children. As public moneys were allocated to pay female teachers' salaries, the functions of the summer schools were gradually integrated into the year-round public grammar school.

Many interesting things might be said about the girls' schools

[7] See "The Republican Mother," in *Women's America: Refocusing the Past*, 2d ed., ed. Linda K. Kerber and Jane De Hart-Mathews (New York: Oxford University Press 1987); Linda K. Kerber, *Women of the Republic: Intellect and Ideology in Revolutionary America* (Chapel Hill: University of North Carolina Press, 1980), chs. 7, 9; "The Republican Mother: Women and the Enlightenment—An American Perspective," *American Quarterly*, 28 (1976): 187–205; "The Republican Ideology of the Revolutionary Generation," *American Quarterly*, 38 (1985): 462–85, 487–88.

of the early Republic: their size; their curricula; their social composition; the extent to which they provided careers open to talented teachers and administrators like Sarah Pierce and Emma Willard; the impact they may have had on notable women of the next generation. Judith Sargent Murray and Benjamin Rush provided very interesting model curricula for these schools and even more interesting justifications for them. They provided the requisite groundwork for a subsequent demand for even more advanced, or "higher," education. Before there could be colleges, there would have to be elementary schools, academies, and seminaries.

These new opportunities were regarded with great ambivalence. They could be welcomed with excitement, but they were also met with profound distrust. Indeed, they became the subject of a bitter debate on the merits of female education. Snippets of this debate—in student essays, in graduation orations, in newspaper columns—hint at the vigor of the argument. The hostility with which educated women were greeted is akin to the skepticism with which upper classes have traditionally regarded the spread of literacy among the poor or to the fear whites displayed for the urge for learning by freed black people after the Civil War. Approval of the new competence was balanced by a fear that new knowledge might make its holders more troublesome. As literate women moved into a male world of print and commerce, they found themselves criticized for transforming the roles that had been theirs by virtue of their gender. They encountered a variant of the anti-intellectualism which Richard Hofstadter identified as a distinctive feature of American life in all such stressful times.[8] This consisted of the assertion that women did not need learning, for they could not be wise, that women's minds were by their nature attracted to the trivial. This idea can be found in Plato when he discusses the women of his own time; it had

[8] Richard Hofstadter, *Anti-Intellectualism in American Life* (New York: Knopf, 1969).

retained its vigor down the long centuries, and it received fresh energy in the years of the early Republic.

The complaint that the learned woman crossed the boundaries of her sex, a complaint lodged against Jane Colman Terrell, was still being made in the early Republic. Indeed, the very fact that it was made shows us, as in mirror image, that women were reaching for access to higher education and gaining enemies in the process. "Women of masculine minds," thundered the Boston minister John Sylvester John Gardiner, "have generally masculine manners, and a robustness of person ill calculated to inspire the tender passion."[9] Addressing a "Lady, Who Expressed A Desire of Seeing a University Established for Women," a contributor to the *American Museum* warned:

> Deluded maid! Thy claim forego [sic]. . . .
> Science has, doubtless, powerful charms,
> But then abjure her tempting arms,
> For shoulds't thou feel her first embrace,
> Farewell to ev'ry winning grace
> Farewell to ev'ry pleasing art
> That binds in chains the yielding heart.[10]

When we find evidence of male undergraduates wrestling with the issue of women's education, we can be sure it had entered general conversation. At the Dartmouth College graduation in 1797 two seniors staged a dialogue:

Mr. Bannister: [Sexual distinction] is arbitrary, because it is not authorized by the least superiority of talents, or merit, or any kind, in our sex over that of the other. Our boasted prerogative is, therefore, wholly assumed, and wholly unjust. . . .
Mr. Little: . . . men have strong intellectual powers, great pene-

[9] *Massachusetts Mercury and New-England Palladium* (Boston), September 18, 1801.
[10] *American Museum* (February 1788).

tration, and solid judgment *[sic]* . . . , women have not so strong intellectual powers but, having greater sensibility, and being more easily persuaded, they are very amiable and pleasing. . . .
Bannister: Mental difference! There is no such thing. . . . [Is it] no disparagement to be considered and treated as an inferior? To be valued only for convenience and utility?
Little: . . . Did you ever hear of a female Demosthenes, or Cicero. . . ?
Bannister: That they have not been generals, orators, statesmen and abstruse philosophers, I must indeed, confess. But this is owing to their education, and confined spheres of action; and not to a want of mental capacities. . . . [As for mathematics and science,] they are taught that those studies do not belong to them; that they are entirely out of their sphere, and that they are dry, hard, and uninteresting; and that, after all, they will be of no advantage to them; but will make them masculine, and ever despised. . . .

In the end Bannister assures Little that his reforms do not go so far as to envision women in the halls of Congress, and reassured, Little concedes defeat: "I have been misguided by common opinion, blinded by prejudice. . . ."[11]

Supreme Court Justice James Iredell's son, a student at Princeton, wrote an essay which expressed some of the same ideas:

Can it . . . be pretended that the intellectual powers of women are inferior, & that the vigour of the mind is increased or diminished by bodily strength or weakness? . . . The strongest [male] minds are often enclosed in the weakest frames. The want of bodily strength thus can be no argument to prove the inferiority of woman in intellectual powers. . . . It is well known that the education of women has ever been & is now generally neglected. . . . If they would cultivate the mind with that assiduity which they bestow on the frivolities of dress . . . , if they would apply themselves to the study of the abstruser sciences, we might have ora-

[11] Dartmouth College Archives.

tors, historians, & philosophers from that sex as well as from the other. . . .[12]

In the early eighteenth century there had been only one respectable position on the subject; by the end of the century, as we see, there were at least two. Mary Wollstonecraft's arguments had been taken by at least one portion of the community to reflect the common sense of the matter. Young men could be found who understood that the limits to female intelligence were more a matter of educational opportunity than of nature. In a few quarters, visions of women's education enlarged. "I think the propriety of circumscribing the education of a female, within such narrow bounds as are frequently assigned, is at least problematic," remarked Judith Sargent Murray. Although she was more than a generation away from Margaret Fuller's demand that "a being of infinite scope must not be treated with an exclusive view to any one relation," the strict limits on what a girl might learn were weakening.

Learning in women even began to be welcomed as a path to an upwardly mobile marriage. The best evidence for this point comes from a graduation skit performed in Greenfield, Massachusetts, in 1800. Fifteen-year-old Sally Ripley played the part of a girl named Nelly, whose words reflected uncritically the attitudes of her traditional family: "Uncle Tristam says he hates to have girls go to school, it makes them so darn'd uppish & so dread proud that they won't work. . . ." Gradually Nelly is persuaded to recognize that educated men speak to educated women with respect. She comes to see schooling as a way to make herself appealing to men who are more refined than "humdrum" farmers. She goes to a dance with the students and finds that she is treated like a lady. "They did not

---

[12] James Iredell, Jr., "On the Female Sex," February 18, 1805, Iredell Papers, University of North Carolina. I am grateful to Don Higginbotham for this reference.

say: come along Nell & here it goes Nell—but shall I have the pleasure to dance with you Miss Nelly. . . . They treated me so well that it really made me feel PURELY." At last she reflects "if I really thought I could get a nice husband I don't know but I should try to larn" and finally decides: "I'll go to school with all my heart. . . . Well now this beat all, that you should by Arithmetic [increase] the likelihood of being married—I'll learn arithmetic, I will, I will."[13]

Moreover, it could be respectable to welcome learning for its own sake. One is struck by the hunger of some women for learning, for access not only to skills but to wisdom, and by their expression of resentment of their exclusion from the world of books. Susanna Rowson wrote in 1794:

> There is no reason why we should stop short in the career of knowledge, though it has been asserted by the other sex that the distaff, the needle, together with domestic concerns alone should occupy the time of women. . . . When literature and the study of fine arts can be engaged in . . . why may we not attain the goal of perfection as well as the other sex? The human MIND, whether possessed by man or woman, is capable of the highest refinement and most brilliant acquirements.[14]

Finally, and perhaps most significantly, learning in women could be welcomed as a route to power and an expression of ambition. In an era in which Jefferson was shocked to find Hamilton acknowledging his hunger for fame frankly and openly, it was the more startling to find Judith Sargent Murray writing that young minds ought to be taught to aspire. Ambition is a noble principle, she argued, and she urged that girls be taught "to reverence themselves . . . that is, their intellectual eminence," insisting that self-respect and intellectual power

[13] Diary of Sally Ripley. Quoted with the permission of the American Antiquarian Society.
[14] *Mentoria: or The Young Ladies Friend* (Philadelphia: N.p., 1794), preface.

went together. She warned against attempts by parents to elim-
inate pride; properly understood, pride (or "self-complacency") seemed to her a useful defense against false flattery
and manipulation by others, especially men.

> Self-estimation, kept within due bounds
> However oddly this assertion sounds,
> May, of the fairest efforts be the root . . .
> May stimulate to most exalted deeds,
> Direct the soul where blooming honor leads.[15]

Another female poet, writing an attack on Alexander Pope,
claimed:

> In either sex the appetites' the same
> For love of power is still the love of fame. . . .
> . . . Power, alike, both males and females love. . . .
> In education all the difference lies;
> Women, if taught, would be as learnd and wise
> As haughty man, improved by arts and rules. . . .[16]

"There are some ambitious spirits," observed Emma Willard
comfortably in 1819, "who cannot be confined in the household and who need a theatre in which to act. . . ." Instead of
being distressed at the possibility of ambition in women, she
proposed that they use their energies to establish and direct
female academies.[17]

A recurrent theme in these prescriptions for women's education was, as Murray had said, that a woman ought to be

[15] Judith Sargent Murray, "Desultory Thoughts upon the Utility of Encouraging a
Degree of Self-Complacency, Especially in Female Bosoms," *Gentlemen and Ladies
Town and Country Magazine* (October 1784): 251–52.

[16] "On Pope's Characters of Women," by a Lady, *American Museum* 9 (1792): 13–
15.

[17] Emma Willard, *An Address to the Public . . . Proposing a Plan for Improving Female
Education* (Middlebury: N.p., 1819): 34.

taught "to reverence herself." Study of history had an important role in this, ever since David Hume in 1741 had commended history as an antidote to novels, which he believed offered "false representations of mankind." But women harbored some skepticism. Miss Morland, in Jane Austen's *Northanger Abbey*, explains why she prefers popular novels to history: "I read it [history] a little as a duty, but it tells me nothing that does not either vex or weary me. The quarrels of popes and kings, with wars or pestilences, in every page; the men all so good for nothing, and hardly any women at all."

If what a woman should study included needlework and cooking, it also included women's history, which linked girls to heroic women of the past and attempted, however hesitantly, to provide for women a place in the civic culture, eroding the antique barriers between the world of men and the world of women. Feminist writers and teachers responded to these demands by compiling lists of accomplished women and anthologies of historical snippets. Women's history as a subject of study in America may be said to have begun with the late-eighteenth-century search for a usable past. Compilers of "Ladies Repositories," ladies' magazines, and textbooks for girls' schools ransacked their libraries, tumbling historical examples about. They were often heedless of chronology: Charlotte Corday might be paired with Lady Jane Grey, Margaret of Anjou with Catherine of Russia. Not until Oberlin's opening years were there coherent histories of American women available for the female audience. Samuel L. Knapp's *Female Biography* did not appear before 1834; Lydia Maria Child's A *History of the Condition of Women in Various Ages and Conditions*, in 1835; Sarah Josepha Hale's *Woman's Record*, in 1853. Elizabeth Ellet's great compilation of the activities of women during the American Revolution appeared in 1848.

Hesitantly, carefully, it became possible for a young woman, growing to maturity in the early nineteenth century, to contemplate advanced education as an attractive option. The curriculum of the girls' seminaries was, of course, not often rigorous; even the "Ladies' Course" at Oberlin would now appear to us to be that of a secondary school rather than a college. But the path of Lucy Stone, which took her from her town school, to rather marginal female seminaries, to Mount Holyoke Female Seminary, and finally to Oberlin, where she became the first Massachusetts woman to take a college degree, epitomizes not only a single woman's own educational quest but one woman's use of institutional options which Jane Colman Terrell could not have imagined.

In the third era, from 1833 to 1885, the number of schools grew steadily—seminaries at a faster pace than colleges. The temptation for the modern observer to tell an institutional story here is very great. It is easy enough to chart intellectual opportunity in terms of the growth in the number of classrooms, teachers, and growing access to professions. But there was an extra-academic, extra-institutional aspect of American intellectual life, as indeed, there still is; it was very strong in the nineteenth century, and it had particular relevance for women.

In a world in which only a few thousand women were in college or university in any given year, most "higher" education was necessarily self-education.[18] Women shaped their intellectual lives out of their own reading, their diary keeping, and their letter writing. Their study was squeezed into the domestic tasks their families—even the most supportive—required of them. "Dear Friend," wrote Sarah Bradford to Mary Moody Emerson in 1814. "You will have me write—what? The interesting detail of mending, sweeping, teaching? What amusement can you reasonably require at the hand of a being

---

[18] The usually cited figures are 11,000 in 1870, but that includes seminaries; 3,000 is closer to the mark for colleges. See Barbara Miller Solomon, *In the Company of Educated Women: A History of Women and Higher Education in America* (New Haven: Yale University Press, 1985): 63, 44; Helen Lefkowitz Horowitz, *Alma Mater: Design and Experience in the Women's Colleges from Their Nineteenth Century Beginnings to the 1930's* (New York: Knopf, 1984).

secluded in a back chamber, with a basket of stockings on one side, and an old musty heathen on the other? Musty! reiterates father Homer, frowning through his gilt cover. . . ."[19] Their study was often undisciplined: years later Sarah Bradford was to recall accurately of her friend, "She has read, all her life, in the most miscellaneous way. . . ." One may be permitted to wonder whether Mary Moody Emerson would have rambled on in her writing had there been a public audience for it as there was for the writing of her brother?

Justifications for study fell into three categories, only two of them considered respectable: religious self-appraisal of the sort especially sanctioned by Calvinist tradition, service to the family by preparing oneself to teach one's children, and self-indulgence. In the private writing of mid-century women we can sense this need for a justification for learning which was self-fulfilling as well as self-indulgent, for a rationale for learning which enabled one to shape one's own self or affect one's own community. This wish and this need could be embeddeed in the act of selecting Mme. de Staël's *Corrine* as one of the most popular novels of the first half of the nineteenth century; in *Corrine*, as almost nowhere else until George Eliot, women could find a vision of a sister who sought to please herself and who made demands on the society of men.[20]

The experiences of Lydia Maria Child and Margaret Fuller suggest some of the pains of trying to structure an intellectual's career without institutional support. Child's formal education extended no further than dame school, though her brother Convers Francis, to whom she was very close, graduated from Harvard and studied at the Harvard Divinity School. Yet she read widely and seriously. At fifteen she was complaining to

[19] Sarah Butler Wister and Agness Irwin, eds., *Worthy Women of Our First Century* (Philadelphia: N.p., 1877): 130.
[20] As Gail Parker has observed, "Madame de Staël had suggested that it was possible for a woman to be Byronic—at least if she were willing to die young." *The Oven Birds: American Women on Womanhood* (New York: Doubleday, 1972): 13.

her brother about "Milton's treatment of our sex" in *Paradise Lost*; at eighteen she was teaching school in Maine and searching for a religious identity, which she found in the Unitarian Church; and at twenty-two she was writing her first novel. *Hobomok: A Tale of Early Times* (1824) was a political fiction which entered assertively into public argumentation about the status of Indians, interracial marriage, and Puritan history. Its success prompted the Boston Athenaeum to offer Child an honorary membership that provided free access to its library, but this institutional relationship was withdrawn a few years later, when she offended conservatives with her trailblazing antislavery pamphlet *An Appeal in Favor of That Class of Americans Called Africans* (1833). Thereafter she would proceed—as did most of her male contemporaries—without institutional support for her studies, finding intellectual and political sustenance in the overlapping communities of transcendentalists and abolitionists, and intellectual support, too, in friendship and dialogue with women who became informal colleagues—Margaret Fuller among them.[21]

Everyone who knew Fuller seems to have agreed that she had a fine mind; she spent much of her life restlessly searching for a context in which to exercise it effectively and consequentially. Unlike Child, she was deeply skeptical of voluntary associations; unlike Catharine Beecher, she found teaching girls' schools deeply frustrating.[22] Her "conversations," an effort to guide the learning of other women, were constructed in criticism of women's educational options; she opened the first session with the following declaration:

> Women are now taught, at school, all that men are; they run over, superficially, even *more* studies, without being really taught

[21] See Milton Meltzer and Patricia C. Holland, eds., *Lydia Maria Child: Selected Letters, 1817–1880* (Amherst, Mass.: University of Massachusetts Press, 1982): chs. 1, 2.
[22] See her letters on teaching in Providence in 1837 in Robert N. Hudspeth, ed., *The Letters of Margaret Fuller* (Ithaca, N.Y.: Cornell University Press, 1983): 1: 288ff.

anything. When they come to the business of life, they find themselves inferior, and all their studies have not given them that practical good sense, and mother wisdom, and wit, which grew up
with our grandmothers at the spinning-wheel. But, with this difference; men are called on, from a very early period, to reproduce
all that they learn. Their college exercises, their political duties,
their professional studies, the first actions of life in any direction,
call on them to put to use what they have learned. But women
learn without any attempt to reproduce. Their only reproduction
is for purpose of display.[23]

Deep into the century the constrained context in which Fuller
had struggled persisted. In 1885 Annie Nathan, an eighteen-
year-old-New York girl, began to read the *Memoirs of Margaret Fuller* and not long thereafter organized a reading group
called the Seven Wise Women. "The idea came to me last
year while reading of M. Fuller's social gatherings. . . . The
idea is to study these women carefully—& write an essay upon
each: Hannah More, Mary Wollstonecraft, E. B. Browning,
Mary Somerville, M. Fuller, Harriet Martineau, Caroline
Herschel, Geo. Eliot."[24]

By 1885 there was a substantial institutional context for the
aspirations of girls like Annie Nathan. She knew of authentic
colleges for women: Vassar was already twenty years old, Smith
and Wellesley had opened ten years before, and Bryn Mawr
was a year old in 1884. The 1870s were something of a "take-
off" decade for coeducational, especially public, institutions.
At the University of Wisconsin and the University of Missouri
women reasserted their claim to a liberal education in the same

[23] In *Memoirs of Margaret Fuller Ossoli* (Boston: Phillips, Sampson, 1852): I: 329. See
Caroline Healey Dall, *Margaret and Her Friends* (Boston: N.p., 1897): 46, for a
description of the series given to an audience of men and women, where Emerson
attempted to monopolize the floor: "Emerson pursued his own train of thought. He
seemed to forget that we had come together to pursue Margaret's."
[24] Papers of Annie Nathan Meyer, Box 12, Folder 5, June 3, October 18, 1885.
American Jewish Archives (AJA), Cincinnati, Ohio.

classes with men, instead of segregated in a normal school; at the University of Michigan a fund-raising campaign to provide the $100,000 necessary to establish the female department promised by the university's charter finally succeeded. In 1885 the Mississippi State College for Women, the first female public institution in the South, opened its doors.[25] In Nathan's own city of New York the options were more constricted, but Columbia College had just established an "Annex" through which women could be examined by Columbia professors, although they could not take courses. Annie Nathan entered this marginal academic setting. Within a few years she had given herself up to a major campaign to endow a women's college. Before five years were up, Barnard College was in existence, and Annie Nathan was writing: "Felt happy and proud to see evidence of my work. I can always look to Barnard College even if I am only 23 & feel if I die tomorrow, I have not lived in vain. I do hope that next year this time we have an endowment of $250,000."[26]

The intensity of young Annie Nathan's feelings about her college experience was characteristic of her generation. College women in the late nineteenth century knew that they had made an unusual commitment; "we worked in those years," Jane Addams recalled of her time at Rockford in the 1870s, "as if we really believed the portentous statement from Aristotle . . . with which we illuminated the wall occupied by our Chess club. . . . There is the same difference between the learned and the unlearned as between the living and the dead."[27] Many felt a strong sense of obligation that their educations be used for some larger social good, but it also began to be possible to be part of a "group of women who have gone on acquiring knowledge for themselves," as one Vassar alumna put it in

---

[25] Solomon, *In the Company of Educated Women*, ch. 4.

[26] Journal of Annie Nathan Meyer, October 6, 1890, Meyer Papers, AJA.

[27] In *Twenty Years at Hull House*, quoted in *The American Woman: Who Was She?*, ed. Anne Firor Scott (Englewood Cliffs, N.J.: Prentice-Hall, 1971): 65–66.

1895, recounting the 118 Vassar alumnae who were involved in or had acquired graduate degrees. By the 1920s the struggles of these women had faded from consciousness. "Never forget," Alice Duer Miller would demand of students at Barnard, "how many people have broken their hearts to get your college for you."

The founding of institutions of higher education for women brings us back to Alice Mary Baldwin. Required by her vulnerable position, as dean of the women's college at Duke, to exercise the greatest discretion, she offered her criticisms of the state of women's education only in passing, leaving them to be read between the lines of passionless accounts of her own college. Occasionally it is possible to see what she really thought. In 1932 she called for "real coordination rather than subordination" when a women's college was part of a university. "There should be women on the board of trustees." The budget should not be wholly in the hands of men. There should be on the faculty "a reasonable number of women of fine personality and ripe scholarship."[28] By 1949 she was complaining that "in the larger coeducational institutions . . . the interests of the women students, always in the minority, tend to be submerged in those of the men. . . . Perhaps the most serious loss is in the part played by the women themselves; in their sense of unity, of belonging to a college which is peculiarly their own and for which they are in large part responsible. . . ." Her posthumous memoir provides the evidence that she knew herself to be undervalued and underpaid throughout her life at Duke, and she was outraged not only for herself but for the women of the college whom she served.

Alice Mary Baldwin's world was far removed from that of Jane Colman Terrell of the eighteenth century, or even of Judith Sargent Murray, Emma Willard, or Margaret Fuller of

---

[28] *Proceedings*, Association of Colleges and Secondary Schools of the Southern States, 1932, in A. M. Baldwin Papers, Duke.

the nineteenth, but one theme linked them all. They all lived
in a culture deeply skeptical of learned women. It is true that
as time went on, women found more and more allies in their
quest for intellectual freedom and opportunity. Skepticism was
voiced with more delicacy; no minister thundered from the
pulpit that the learned woman was necessarily masculine. But
people still viewed people such as Alice Baldwin as oddities.
As a learned woman she was still in some sense a "bluestock-
ing"; and few would be surprised that she never married. Baldwin's memoir shows that, though she spent her entire life at
Duke, she knew she was not welcomed to fellowship with her
male colleagues, and it hurt. Perhaps I am overly optimistic,
but I believe that in our generation this cultural constant is at
last being erased and that it will be eradicated in our lifetime.
This erasure is marked by the absorption of women into previously masculine professions and institutions and by changes
in patterns of courtesy. It is because it is coming to the end of
its life that we can finally take a distanced view of it, finally
see it as an ideological position, rather than as the common
sense of the matter.

For 200 years it was assumed that higher education for men
and for women could not be quite the same. Women had to
find room for their educations without eliciting male hostility
and contempt. It was assumed that the course of study for
women required special justification; the standard question was,
What studies are appropriate for the female mind? Adam Smith
said that what women needed was a continuation of what had
been learned in the home and could be used directly and prac-
tically in adult life; he called for "no absurdities." In the nineteenth century the list of appropriate studies lengthened; it
became respectable for women to contemplate a widening range
of activities. But few would say with Margaret Fuller, "[L]et
them be sea-captains if they will," and fewer still would maintain that women might properly indulge in any form of study.
As recently as 1956 it was fresh and unusual for Harvard soci-

ologist David Riesman to propose for women an education that would be *discontinuous* with what had come before, that would "put pressure on life," open up new worlds of learning, encourage new ambitions, make room for the problematic and, in Adam Smith's word, the "fantastical."[29] When the Ivy League colleges opened their doors to women in the 1970s, they answered firmly that question by taking Riesman's, and Judith Sargent Murray's, and Margaret Fuller's positions: All studies are appropriate for the female mind; no one need any longer fear undermining her own character by what she chooses to study.

But if we have resolved in this generation the question of whether women's minds are fit for serious thought, we have not yet fully resolved the related issue of whether women's experience is as important a part of our cultural inheritance as the medieval cathedral, of whether it is as important for men to study women's experience as it has been for women to study men's. The revolution that is women's studies addresses that issue. The educational challenge before us is to transform our institutions of higher education so that they not only accept both men and women as students but also provide for both an understanding of the world in which the record of women's experience, needs, and accomplishments is regarded with as much respect and as much pride as the record of men. The story of Jane Colman Terrell is not of interest because it was "quaint" but because she was silenced. Her story is as much a part of American educational history as the story of Harvard College. Alice Mary Baldwin was seeking to find a way to tell us this when she died. I think she would be pleased to know that many voices have now been added to hers.

[29] David Riesman, "Continuities and Discontinuities in Women's Education," Bennington College Commencement Address, 1956.

JOYCE ANTLER

The Educational Biography of Lucy Sprague Mitchell: A Case Study in the History of Women's Higher Education

For generations of women the opportunity to go to college has been an enabling, energizing force, stimulating talent, nurturing self-esteem, developing skills and competencies. Perhaps Mary Emma Woolley, president of Mount Holyoke College, had this quality in mind when she noted in 1919 that "The higher education of women is a feministic movement, the natural expression of a fundamental principle that is that women being first of all human beings, even before they are feminine, have a share in the inalienable right of human beings to self-development."[1]

Yet the experience of college has been educative to women in distinctly different ways from that of men. Women have

[1] Jeanette Marks, *Life and Letters of Mary Emma Woolley* (Washington, D.C.: Public Affairs Press, 1955): 80.

JOYCE ANTLER *is professor of education at Brandeis University, Waltham, Massachusetts.*

had less access to higher education than men. They have studied separate bodies of knowledge in sex-segregated classrooms; even the pedagogies that taught men and women have frequently been different. The opportunities available to women after college have been far fewer than those open to men. Equally important, the expectations that women have formed of higher education have differed in significant ways from those of men. These differences have only recently been documented, a product of the movement to bring women's experience to a historical record that has almost always excluded it.[2]

While the education of college women has been limited by discriminatory practices as well as the traditional ideology of separate spheres, the opportunities which colleges have provided for rigorous intellectual training and peer sociability have nevertheless helped foster women's independence, stimulate their ambitions, and develop their aspirations for leadership. The new scholarship in the history of women suggests that even when women have suffered the tensions, confusions, provocations, and hostilities of gender-biased education, they have been able to use aspects of their training in the interests of broad social and political change or, more frequently, for personal growth.

To understand the richness and diversity of women's expe-

---

[2] Among the most important new works in the higher education of women are Charlotte W. Conable, *Women at Cornell: The Myth of Equal Education* (Ithaca, N.Y.: Cornell University Press, 1977); Roberta Frankfort, *Collegiate Women: Domesticity and Career in Turn-of-the-Century America* (New York: New York University Press, 1977); Helen Lefkowitz Horowitz, *Alma Mater: Design and Experience in the Women's Colleges from Their Nineteenth Century Beginnings to the 1930s* (New York: Knopf, 1984); Florence Howe, *Myths of Coeducation: Selected Essays, 1964–1983* (Bloomington, Ind.: Indiana University Press, 1984); Patricia Palmieri, "In Adamless Eden: A Social Portrait of the Academic Community at Wellesley College, 1875–1920" (Ed. E. thesis, Harvard Graduate School of Education, 1981); Pamela Perun, ed., *The Undergraduate Woman: Issues in Educational Equity* (Lexington, Mass.: Lexington Books, 1982); Margaret Rossiter, *Women Scientists in America* (Baltimore: Johns Hopkins University Press, 1982); and Barbara Miller Solomon, *In the Company of Educated Women* (New Haven: Yale University Press, 1984).

rience of higher education during this past century, historians must elevate the personal impact college has had upon women's lives. Elucidation of the subjective dimensions of student experience—the ways in which education aided an individual in personally integrating her powers and abilities and in finding her place in social, cultural, and political life and the world of work—can help historians understand changes in the larger meanings of higher education over time. The general patterns of higher eduction as a force for continuous lifetime learning inside and outside the classroom may be gleaned through biographical studies, on both an individual and a collective basis.

My research on Lucy Sprague Mitchell (1878–1967), progressive educator, administrator, and writer, illustrates the use of educational biography in interpreting women's educational history.[3] Mitchell's experience provides an example of the varied influences which combine to shape a college learning environment—among them pedagogy, curriculum, social life, residence patterns, role models, personalities, and ideology. Her educational biography tells us that to understand student experience, we must look at what Mitchell called "intake"— the message students received from this complex environ ment—as well as "outgo"—the concrete, individual ways in which received information was synthesized and utilized in the formation of personal values and expectations.

Mitchell's educational biography also provides an unusual opportunity to examine three different contexts of higher education: a single sex (coordinate) school, a coeducational university, and a teacher training school. Mitchell graduated from Radcliffe College in 1900, then, when she was twenty-eight years old, became the first dean of women and one of the first

---

[3]On the definition and construction of educational biography, see Ellen Condliffe Lagemann, *A Generation of Women: Education in the Lives of Progressive Reformers* (Cambridge: Harvard University Press, 1979). On Lucy Sprague Mitchell, see my *Lucy Sprague Mitchell: The Making of a Modern Woman* (New Haven: Yale University Press, 1987).

female faculty members at the University of California, a position she held until 1912. Finding neither of these environments congenial to her own career aspirations or to the ambitions of educated women generally, she left higher education for what she felt was the more significant arena of early-childhood education. She established the Bureau of Experimental Education in 1916 and, as part of the bureau, the Cooperative School for Teachers in 1931. The bureau was informally called "Bank Street" when it moved to 69 Bank Street in Greenwich Village in 1930, and it officially became the Bank Street College of Education in 1951. Under Mitchell's guidance, Bank Street played a major role in bringing "progressive" notions of schooling—a concern for individual development, the encouragement of curiosity and understanding rather than rote learning, and, above all, a respect for the child's own pleasure in activity—into the mainstream of education.

In choosing the field of so many of the pioneer women educators of the nineteenth century—teacher training—Mitchell demonstrated the link twentieth-century educators forged with earlier generations of women. Her creation of a radically different kind of normal school curriculum, however, reflected her dissatisfaction with both the traditional masculine and feminine models of professional education. As we shall see, Mitchell's education perspectives had been shaped in large part by the patterns of discrimination and sex segregation which she experienced as a student, teacher, and administrator. Gradually she came to understand the meaning of gender as it affected her college experiences and life choices. Her mature career at Bank Street, which was largely based on bringing the "primaries" of poetry and humanity into public and institutional life, built upon this insight.

Though her educational biography suggests patterns relevant to the experiences of many women of her generation, Mitchell herself came from a highly privileged background. Lucy Sprague was born in 1878 to Otho Sprague, a wealthy

Chicago merchant, and his wife, Lucia. During her childhood and adolescence the fortunate economic circumstances of her family seemed more of a burden than an opportunity. A lonely and repressed girl who chafed under her father's rigid discipline, Lucy never attended school on a regular basis until she was sixteen. Whenever she was sent to school, she always broke down. "I twitched constantly and uncontrollably and had these terrible pains in my legs," she recalled.[4] Tutored at home until she was twelve, she read her way, shelf by shelf, around her father's voluminous classical library, specializing in works of history and archaeology. But she regretted her isolation from her peers and, by early adolescence, had come to separate herself as well from her family's attitudes and lifestyle. She believed that her father's materialism was the cause of his growing hostility to settlement leader Jane Addams, whom he had formerly supported, since Addams sympathized with striking Chicago laborers.

After the Spragues moved to Southern California in 1893, Lucy entered the Marlborough School, a girls' private preparatory academy in Los Angeles. Though the Marlborough School was designed to give elite young women training in social deportment, for Lucy it provided the context for intellectual excellence and scholarly achievement. Headmistress Mary Caswell encouraged Lucy's plans for college and helped her with preparatory exams for Radcliffe. Only one other Marlborough student graduating before 1900 went on to college.

"Rich girls were sent to 'finishing school,'" Lucy later recalled, while "a girl who wanted to go to college [was] looked up as a little queer . . . unfeminine . . . stuck up."[5] Indeed, her father strongly opposed her desire to attend college; her

---

[4] Lucy Sprague Mitchell, *Two Lives, The Story of Wesley Clair Mitchell and Myself* (New York: Simon & Schuster, 1953): 58.
[5] Lucy Sprague Mitchell Papers, Rare Book and Manuscript Library, Columbia University.

insistence on leaving home in the face of his disapproval was her first concrete act of rebellion against her family.

Lucy Sprague was an exemplary student at Radcliffe, where she studied philosophy with William James, Josiah Royce, and George Santayana, becoming the first Radcliffe student to receive honors in that subject. Sprague was active in athletics and drama and served as class vice-president as well as class historian. Despite these achievements, her Radcliffe experience was mixed. Most Harvard professors, if not her own philosophy teachers, treated women students with a mixture of respect, contempt, and condescension. Some of them had been unalterably opposed to the establishment of the coordinate women's college, Radcliffe, feeling that it could become "a vampire, sucking the lifeblood of the university."[6] Others treated women if not superciliously then differently, regarding them as delicate creatures of femininity, rather than simply as qualified students.[7] Radcliffe women taking Harvard classes were troubled not only by the attitudes of professors but also by the general social constraints of campus life. A classmate of Lucy's described the atmosphere at Radcliffe at the turn of the century:

> From the moment I entered Radcliffe . . . I was forbidden to go to the Square, not even if I needed something at the Coop. Of course, I never had been allowed in the Yard except well chaperoned. I had two cousins in Harvard at this time, and they threatened me that if I ever disobeyed this rule they'd contrive to find it out and "fix" me. It was bad enough, they contended, to have the disgrace of a cousin at Radcliffe, without running the risk of meeting her on the street (and being obliged to cut her).

[6] William Byerly, "Radcliffe College Thirty Years After," *Harvard Graduate Magazine* (December 1909): 5.
[7] Lewis Gates, who taught the English composition course Lucy and her classmates were required to take, told his students, for example, that " women are lyrical interludes in man's strenuous existence," a statement that they mocked but resented.

Going to the Harvard Library was an equally formidable experience for this student. When one professor sent her to Harvard Library to work on her senior thesis, she persuaded her grandmother that her "entire future depended on my standing well with Prof Baker. . . . Grandmother accepted the necessity, and accompanied me to the library. I can feel the whole scene now:—my own hot shame lest someone should see me . . . and Grandmother, uncomfortably knitting on one of the hard wooden chairs in the little upstairs alcove . . . sighing unconsciously now and then, but steadfast until my work was finished."[8] The general avoidance of public places where women students might mix with men became standard rituals to protect and secure female propriety, to be disobeyed only at the cost of incurring personal humiliation. Radcliffe's status was relatively unusual, but similar patterns of interaction between men and women existed at coeducational schools in the late nineteenth and twentieth centuries.[9]

The attitudes of Radcliffe's women officials toward the rules and rituals to be followed by Radcliffe girls were scarcely better than those of the Harvard faculty. Even Radcliffe's president, Elizabeth Agassiz, treated students as delicate creatures whose femininity needed careful protection.

We had . . . the same examinations as the Lords of Creation lasting something over three hours. On one occasion, Mrs. Agassiz wandered into the room and saw me at work. She came up and tentatively asked me if I wasn't working too hard. I put my finger on my lips, shook my head, and pointed to the Proctor.

[8] Lucy Fuller, January 27, 1934, in *My Tenth Anniversary*, Ada Comstock Scrapbook, Radcliffe College Archives, Radcliffe College.
[9] See, for example, Conable, *Women at Cornell*; Lynn D. Gordon, "Coeducation on Two Campuses: Berkeley and Chicago, 1890–1912," in *Woman's Being, Woman's Place: Female Identity and Vocation in American History*, ed. Mary Kelley (Boston: G. K. Hall, 1979); Patricia F. Haines, "For Honor and Alma Mater: Perspectives on Coeducation at Cornell University, 1868–1885," *Journal of Education* 159 (August 1977); and Howe, *Myths of Coeducation*.

"What is the matter?" she asked. I said, "You mustn't talk to me. He'll think you're helping me." "Bless you, my dear," she laughed. "He knows I don't know enough to help you." She moved about through the room for a few moments, and then wandered out. Presently arrived some cups of hot soup, with instructions from her that girls ought not to work so long without nourishment.[10]

Mrs. Agassiz's bouillon at midyear examinations became a fond memory for many Radcliffe students.

The rules of Radcliffe's dean, Agnes Irwin, reinforced the tradition of delicate femininity to be upheld by college girls. Irwin was strenuously opposed to athletic events, which made her students susceptible to injury and strain and, even worse, shot Radcliffe girls into the public press, especially when they were victorious. Irwin also worried about the dramatic appearances of her students; she insisted that actors playing ladies' parts wear costumes down to their ankles, while those who played men's parts at theater events had to conceal their lower limbs in ballooning bloomers. There were even rules for daily excursions: Girls were forbidden to walk outside with their arms around each other; white gloves were always to be worn.

The rules of propriety established by Radcliffe officers, in combination with the daily humiliations inflicted on female students by Harvard men, suggested to Lucy Sprague that women were a distinct class of persons, different from, and certainly not as priviliged as, male students. Female students had always to be on duty and watchful, ever seeking to cloak their behavior in the tenets of true womanhood. Neither boldness nor spontaneity but, instead, invisibility and guardedness were demanded by Radcliffe's informal curriculum. Unfortunately the constraints that Harvard imposed on women students led them to identify with the standards of the superior lot—Harvard men—in the way that less privileged groups often internalize the morality of those with greatest power. Student

[10] *Ibid.*

correspondence and alumnae questionnaires reveal that the majority of students treasured the Harvard connection. The stimulation, the intellectual freedom, and the discipline of scholarship that their access to Harvard's fine faculty gave them could not have been obtained at other schools, they believed. When, on occasion, a Radcliffe student protested women's subordinate status at the university, her classmates usually dissociated themselves from the rebellion. Denying the message of second-class citizenship, students thus selected from their Radcliffe experience those elements that could be most functional in their lives. For many women, Radcliffe did indeed provide a useful context for after-college lives of involvement, caring, and concern, whether within or outside the home. But for others, the failure to confront the discriminatory aspects of an education that was in many respects gender-linked simply masked the ambivalent messages of that education.

The experience of being a Radcliffe-Harvard woman thus created high expectations for undergraduates, but it offered little preparation that might allow them to lead the active lives which they desired. Instead, it gave them a nagging sense of their difference from, and perhaps their inferiority to, men. Many Radcliffe women were to hold themselves accountable when they failed to produce the achievements which they desired.

At the same time Radcliffe also provided students with the opportunities to develop their interests, powers, and responsibilities by directing their own affairs at the college. Later Mitchell was to write, "It is unquestionable that in a coeducational college, where the responsibility of social activities, and consequently the interests in these activities, falls in a lesser degree to the women, that the women develop self-possession less markedly than in the separate college, where they bear the undivided burden."[11] In this respect Radcliffe was a female

<hr>

[11] Lucy Sprague, "The Forms and Results of Student Social Activities," *Journal of the Association of Collegiate Alumnae* 3 (1908): 50–53.

world, which in fact sometimes led to the empowerment of students, however in conflict with other lessons learned by Harvard women.

Lucy Sprague evaluated her experience at Radcliffe both positively and negatively. A half century after graduation she was asked by the college's alumnae organization to describe benefits she had received from Radcliffe. She listed three: first, "getting free" from the narrow world of her family; second, finding new intellectual interests; and third, a general gain in self-confidence, which she felt equipped her to take on new responsibilities after college. No matter the message of subordination which she had keenly felt, Sprague was able to take considerable advantage of Radcliffe as a dynamic social and intellectual world. Nevertheless, on other occasions she recalled sadly that never once in any of her classes did she hear the word *child* or *mother* mentioned, nor was the topic of sexuality or gender ever discussed. On one level such a statement reflects her desire to legitimate her choice of childhood education as a career. Yet it also corresponds to the arguments she made in numerous lengthy papers written for her philosophy classes at Radcliffe, in which she disputed the ideas of her teachers— among them William James, George Herbert Palmer, Hugo Münsterberg, and Josiah Royce—on the subject of free will versus determinism. Sprague's student themes challenged the notions of freedom and individuality held by these leading philosophers on the ground that they excluded her own experience—women's experience—from the sphere of their moral universe. Though many illustrations which they drew upon in their work were gender-neutral, still the foundations and context of their moral analysis had as their center a male-oriented perspective of life and thought. The world of female experience was not regarded as an appropriate sphere for philosophical inquiry or, for that matter, for examination in any other discipline. Lucy Sprague found a curriculum which ignored women's lives to be seriously deficient; in large part because of this reason, she rejected the advice of Josiah Royce to work for a Ph.D. and become a teacher of philosophy.

Even as she categorically denied the existence of freedom of will, Sprague's rejection of the teachings of her esteemed instructors ironically exhibited her own healthy freedom of intellect. Such a confrontational, confident, demanding intellectual posture was unusual for any young college student, male or female. Beyond this personal characteristic, this incident alerts historians of higher education to begin to examine the interaction of students with the subject matter of their education. In this case we see that three-quarters of a century before the launching of the women's studies movement, on an individual, if not a collective basis, women recognized that the frameworks of knowledge upon which their education rested were tainted by a masculine bias.[12] Questioning the basic tenets of Harvard's celebrated new philosophies of empiricism and pragmatism (and, not incidentally, the authority of its creators), Sprague posed an important, if quiet, challenge to the construction of knowledge itself. Her caution about the universality of Harvard's epistemological frameworks suggests that we ought to search harder as we probe the history of women's higher education to locate similar examples of women's far from passive responses to their educations.

Rejecting a career in academic philosophy, Sprague worked briefly doing administrative work at Radcliffe, and then, in 1903, at the invitation of Benjamin Ide Wheeler, president of the University of California, one of the nation's largest coeducational schools, she came to Berkeley "to do something with the women students," as Wheeler put it. She was officially appointed dean of women in 1906. At Berkeley she found the conditions confronting women students even worse that those

---

[12] In *Beyond Separate Spheres: Intellectual Roots of Modern Feminism* (New Haven: Yale University Press, 1982), Rosalind Rosenberg analyzes the challenge made by women graduate students at the University of Chicago and Columbia University to Victorian notions of sexual identity.

at Harvard: Women were isolated on campus, barred from male-run social and political activities, and restricted to a narrow teacher training curricula to the exclusion of other interests. As dean and as one of two female faculty members at the university she tried to resolve these problems through such measures as developing housing and vocational possibilities for female students, encouraging the formation of female organizations, and creating an all-women pageant on the subject of women's contributions to history. This "masque of maidenhood," or Partheneia, as it came to be called, named after the sacrifice of virgins at the Greek Parthenon, continued as an annual women's event at Berkeley until the 1930s.

Nevertheless, Lucy Sprague remained dissatisfied with the options available for women at the University of California. In spite of her innovations, she felt that a combination of limited aspirations, ill-suited academic programs, male hostility, and lack of institutional facilities made Berkeley's women students drab and apathetic. Part of her dismay lay in her own class bias; even though the majority of Radcliffe as well as Berkeley students had come to college to prepare themselves for careers as teachers, she considered the young women from California's mining towns and farms much less studious but more narrowly practical-minded than Radcliffe's earnest "girls." Sprague's respect for the teaching profession also made her critical of women who chose it because of lack of appropriate options. She devoted some of her efforts as dean of women to developing an academic agenda that would provide vocational alternatives to female students.

The disapproval of male faculty toward her own appointment and that of the sole other female professor, Jessica Peixotto, was equally disillusioning. "It was to be expected that the great majority of the faculty should look askance—to put it mildly—at appointing a blooming, inexperienced, and not very intellectual young woman to the faculty," she wrote of the reaction of male colleagues to her own appointment. But, she protested, "Jessica Peixotto was their equal in training and in intelligence, and they acted the same way toward her appointment because she was a woman."[13] Because of their colleagues' hostility, Sprague and Peixotto never attended a faculty meeting. Lucy acknowledged that "Certainly we could have gone, but I know that it would have prejudiced the men against us, and we already had enough to live down."[14]

Shocked by the animosity of male students to female coeds, now Lucy Sprague confronted the realization that male antagonism to educated women was not merely an adolescent phenomenon. She wrote:

> In the course of my work, I came to realize the standards that our culture . . . held for women in education and in the general management of their own lives. I had long been kicking against these standards in my personal life but with no clear analysis of what so frustrated me. It came as a shock when I realized that most of the faculty thought of women frankly as inferior beings. The older men were solidly opposed to having any women on the faculty. Any woman who, intellectually, could hold such a position must be a freak and "unwomanly." To be sure, most of the Harvard faculty held the same opinion, and Radcliffe's creed concerning teachers was "no women" because Harvard had none. . . .[15]

After a decade at the University of California, Sprague rejected an offer from Nicholas Murray Butler, president of Columbia University, to become a candidate for the job of

[13] Sprague, *Two Lives:* 193. Peixotto graduated from the University of California in 1894, earning a Ph.D. in economics from the university in 1900. She was appointed instructor in sociology in 1904 and promoted to assistant professor in 1907. In 1918 she became full professor, the first woman at the university to hold this rank.

[14] Lucy Sprague Mitchell, "Pioneering in Education," oral history conducted in 1960 by Irene M. Prescott, Regional Oral History Office, Bancroft Library, University of California, Berkeley, 1962: 41.

[15] Sprague, *Two Lives:* 192–93.

dean of Barnard College. Instead, she decided to leave the world of higher education entirely, finding it too abstract and remote from the lives and interests of her women students. Her aim was to become dean of women at a high school so that she might provide students with information completely lacking in the college curricula with which she had worked: information about sexuality, love and marriage, childbearing.

In 1912 she resigned her job at the university and, after marrying economist Wesley Clair Mitchell, came to New York City to pursue her interest in the education of children. In 1916, with financial backing from her cousin Elizabeth Sprague Coolidge, she established the Bureau of Educational Experiments, run cooperatively by a twelve-member Working Council which she chaired. In its first years the bureau developed innovative approaches to sex education, promoted the work of New York's Gary League, and was involved in a wide variety of other experimental projects: a farm labor camp, public school nutrition, day nurseries, rural schools, vocational education, intelligence testing, and the development of play materials. Among its most significant achievements were the establishment in 1919 of the first American nursery school for children from birth to three years of age and the development of a curriculum for the early primary grades which ignored traditional gender role patterns. Boys and girls alike dressed in overalls, played with dolls, built trains, trucks, and airplanes, served as captains, pilots, and firemen.[16]

In 1931 Mitchell established the Cooperative School for Student Teachers (CSST) to train teachers to work in the

[16] Earlier "day nurseries" were designed to provide custodial care for the children of working mothers. In contrast, the nursery school of the Bureau of Educational Experiments aimed to stimulate the intellectual, social, and psychological growth of infants and toddlers, while at the same time conducting scientific research into the parameters of children's development. Its dual focus on education and research set it apart from other progressive preschools. See Joyce Antler, "Progressive Education and the Scientific Study of the Child: An Analysis of the Bureau of Education Experiment" *Teachers College Record* 83 (1982): 559–591.

growing number of experimental schools in the New York metropolitan region. The CSST was an unconventional training institution. Practice teaching was at the core of the curriculum; students were placed from Monday through Thursday in one of eight experimental schools, where they actively participated in classroom work. From Thursday to Saturday they attended classes and seminars at Bank Street. In order to release creative sensibilities, they took workshops in painting, drama, and dance. They learned about social issues by visiting New York tenements, health clinics, political rallies, and labor unions. For half a semester they also took internships with such radical political groups as the League for Industrial Democracy and the League of Women Shoppers. In the spring students spent two weeks on a "long trip," usually to Appalachia, visiting coal mines, steel mills, and community institutions in order to learn about workers in unfamiliar cultures and to develop insights into how they themselves might work for social change. At Bank Street they took classes with Lucy Mitchell on environment and language, learning how children think and learning to teach and write for them at their various stages of growth. Courses on child development, observation and recording, and curricula for experimental schools rounded out the offerings. There were no courses on pedagogical methods.

In 1943 Mitchell and several colleagues began a workshop in a Harlem public school to train teachers in the same experimental techniques taught to the schoolteachers she trained at Bank Street. For Mitchell, the extension of progressive school philosophy and practice to the city's public schools fulfilled a long-standing goal. The workshops had a significant impact on the quality of teaching in New York and served as a model for similar efforts elsewhere.

This summary of Lucy Mitchell's educational history allows us to reflect upon the impact of college education on the course of a single individual's life. First, Mitchell's biography reveals how difficult it was even for talented, well-educated, and well-connected women to use their educations outside the home. It took Lucy Sprague Mitchell many years to admit her own drive for independence and intellectual achievement. Her sense of inferiority and lack of training, coupled with the hostility toward intellectual women she encountered, interfered with the expression and shaping of her aspirations. Neither Radcliffe nor the University of California had given her significant encouragement. At the turn of the century most colleges—especially the liberal arts women's schools—provided little concrete support for those interested in professional work. Indeed, the notion of a planned, vertical career, systematically related to college and professional education, had little relevance in these years to women's lives.

The dilemma of marriage versus career was particularly troublesome to Mitchell, as it was to other college women. During the early twentieth century women educators often shared the assumptions of their male colleagues that marriage and motherhood, rather than a professional career, were the proper future for college women. Others recognized that many alumnae would prefer self-supporting work to marriage, but always there was the acknowledgment, as Ethel Puffer Howes once phrased it, of that "persistent vicious alternative—marriage or career."[17]

The tendency of college alumnae to marry and to work seems to have increased significantly in the decade from 1910 to 1920, when somewhere from 10 to 20 percent of married educated women were employed. Many of these women stopped working after the birth of the first child and resumed employment only after the completion of child rearing.[18] Nevertheless by the 1920s it was clear that a large and growing number of

[17] Ethel Puffer Howes, "Accepting the Universe," *Atlantic Monthly* 129 (1922): 445.
[18] Mary E. Cookingham, "Combining Marriage, Motherhood and Jobs Before World War II: Women College Graduates, Classes of 1905–1935," *Journal of Family History* 9 (1984): 179.

educated women were sympathetic to the possibilities of combining marriage and career.[19]

For Lucy Sprague Mitchell, unifying her personal life as wife and mother with her professional work was part of a carefully designed strategy, facilitated by her fortunate economic circumstances. Before she agreed to marry Wesley Clair Mitchell, she and Mitchell had analyzed the question of a married woman's career options in a candid courtship correspondence. After they had moved to New York, she purchased a number of adjoining brownstone buildings in Greenwich Village which served as the Mitchell home as well as the headquarters of the Bureau of Educational Experiments and the site of the City and County School, which her four children attended and where she taught. "We tried to face the situation realistically," she recalled, "and to plan a practical pattern that would give us a genuine group life as a family and also give a good life to each individual member—child or grownup."[20] She added:

> I learned to keep my hands busy most of the time. I carried my sewing with me everywhere, for I made nearly all of the children's clothes . . . and darned all the stockings for four active children and [husband] Robin. . . . I sewed steadily through all committee meetings and even invented a bag with a big wooden hoop, inside of which I could darn stockings on the subway unseen. . . . I learned to do my writing by snatches and to scribble every free moment. . . . As for years I was always up at six to nurse a baby or give a bottle of orange juice, I formed the habit of going to bed to write until the family breakfast at eight. And I planned my outside work so that much of it could be done at home, though I

---

[19] Of 2,000 respondents to a Radcliffe alumnae survey in 1927, 14 percent reported that they were certain marriage and a career could be combined and 50 percent hoped it was possible. Only 9 percent were currently married and working at the time of the survey. See Barbara Miller Solomon, *In the Company of Educated Women* (New Haven: Yale University Press, 1984).

[20] Mitchell, *Two Lives*: 258.

did manage somehow to keep a half-time teaching job going with only a few weeks off for a new baby.[21]

While Mitchell's solution to the problem of unifying marriage and career was an individual rather than a social one, and dependent on her personal wealth, in developing educationally sound preschools and adventuresome teacher training programs, she helped create institutions that allowed other, less privileged women to pursue their work. One commentator noted in 1926 that the nursery school movement, which Mitchell and her colleague Harriet Merrill Johnson did much to stimulate, was the "first glimmering of an educational revolution which [might] ultimately take most women out of the home."[22]

While Mitchell's move from a top administrative post in a major university to the typical female job of elementary school teacher was idiosyncratic, her selection of teaching as a career parallels the occupational choice of the majority of educated women in the late nineteenth and most of the twentieth centuries, and gives us further clues to the effect of college training on individual lives. Teaching has usually been defined as a "semi-professional" rather than professional occupation with little status, authority, or power; the subordinate role of women teachers in educational bureaucracies has been amply documented. Whereas male teachers have tended to advance in educational hierarchies, classroom teaching has usually been the terminal point for women.[23]

[21] Ibid.: 259. "Robin" was a pet name for Mitchell's husband.
[22] Eunice Fuller Barnard, "The Child Takes a Nurse," *The Survey* 57 (December 1, 1926): 326.
[23] See, for example, Amitai Etzioni, *The Semi-Professions and Their Organization: Teachers, Nurses, Social Workers* (New York: Free Press, 1979); David Tyack and Elizabeth Hansot, *Managers of Virtue: Public School Leadership in America, 1820–1980* (New York: Basic Books, 1982): 180–201; Sari Knopp Biklen and Marilyn B. Branigan, eds., *Women and Educational Leadership* (Lexington, Mass.: Lexington Books, 1980); and Sharon Lee Rich and Ariel Phillips, *Women's Experience and Education* (Cambridge: Harvard Educational Review Reprint Series, 1985).

The work of Mitchell and her colleagues in education suggests that we need to revise some of the traditional notions about women teachers. Mitchell never viewed her own advancement or that of her colleagues in the profession as dependent upon the acquisition of administrative authority. She considered classroom teaching a creative, experimental, and scientific endeavor, to be pursued ardently over the course of a continuing career. In her view, teachers were active learners who expanded their personal horizons continuously, at the same time that they aided the larger cause of social reconstruction. Her aim was to train female as well as male teachers who would develop both "a scientific attitude" and "the attitude of the artist" toward their work and their lives. This meant, she wrote, "an attitude of eager, alert observations; . . . of relish, of emotional drive, a genuine participation in some creative phase of work; . . . an experimental, critical and ardent approach. . . ."[24] Teachers who could express themselves freely and learn from experience were "whole" people. They would create "whole" children, who would in turn transform society into a cooperative, democratic commonwealth.

Thus conceived as integral to the work of social reform, the profession of teaching may be interpreted more as a "radical" rather than a conservative career for women, as has usually been the case.[25] Mitchell and her colleagues in the progressive education movement were probably to the left of the majority of teachers in their political beliefs, and more experimental in their methods. Yet many mainstream teachers in the postsuffrage era did share Mitchell's Deweyite notion that education was the basic matrix of social reform. The activities of these educators in the 1920s and 1930s suggest that social reform

---

[24] Mitchell, *Two Lives:* 470.
[25] See Redding Sugg, *Motherteacher: The Feminization of American Education* (Charlottesville, Va.: University Press of Virginia, 1978). Geraldine Clifford has written about the link between teaching as a career for women and public and political activism. See "The Female Teacher and the Feminist Movement," typescript.

goals in education did not die after World War I but were modified by newer modes of scientific professionalism. We might properly regard these teachers as descendants of the women social reformers of the Progressive Era.

Mitchell's educational theory and practice were derived in large part from her own experiences in higher education. Out of the diverse and sometimes conflicting messages she received as a college student, dean, and faculty member, she fashioned an institutional context appropriate to the new kinds of learning and teaching she wanted to encourage. Like Emma Willard, Catharine Beecher, and Mary Lyon, she learned the lesson that women's education need not be shaped along the lines of traditional masculine models. But a century's distance from the ideology of these pioneer educators allowed her to reject the separatist philosophy that had structured their ideals as well as those of the founders and administrators of the first colleges for women a generation later. By the 1930s Mitchell and her colleagues did not need to legitimate their educational and professional objectives through the espousal of a unique, female temperament rooted in biological differences. They believed that women ought to be trained for careers in teaching because teaching was highly significant, difficult work for which scientific preparation was needed, not because women were natural nurturers. At Bank Street Mitchell put back into education that connection to life so characteristic of women's world and the women's professions yet customarily devalued within higher education: the concerns of women—sexuality, childbearing, and child development. The content she had missed in her own college years became an integral part of the curriculum. Mitchell's insistence that education ought to be directed toward life, not just theory, provides one example of the alternative values which a woman-centered higher education offered to students.

Mitchell's work in education exemplifies the way in which alumnae could transform their own lives as they actively shaped and redirected their educations to create new ideas and programs, whether in education, social reform work, medicine, or other professional pursuits. Although relatively few colleges deliberately encouraged women's productive scholarship or the social uses of scholarship in the late nineteenth and early twentieth centuries, exposure to the higher learning led many women to conceive of themselves in new ways and fostered creative thinking about intellectual and social problems. Despite discriminatory, sex-segregated programs, higher education could, and did, serve as an activating force in women's lives.

LINDA M. PERKINS
The Education of Black Women in the Nineteenth Century

Formal higher education for all Americans in the first half of the nineteenth century was a rarity. Despite the 200-year history of American colleges and universities by that time, it made little economic sense to attend college in the nineteenth century. Such education was indeed seen as a frill, and the "educated man" of the period could gain knowledge by private tutors, personal travels, or self-education. Thus, opportunities were limited for the average white male. For blacks and women, however, such opportunities were often legally as well as socially prohibited prior to the Civil War.

The appropriateness and purposes of education for blacks and white women, who were overwhelmingly viewed by society as intellectually inferior to white men, created great debate

LINDA M. PERKINS *is a visiting scholar at the Center for Afro-American Studies, University of California, Los Angeles.*

during the early decades of the nineteenth century. The prevailing view of society was that neither group should be educated at all. However, some members of the nation argued that both groups should at least be educated to fulfill adequately their prescribed place in society—the good and dutiful white wife and mother and the respectable and humble black person. Thus, "female" and "Negro" education emerged. Both types of education dictated that members of these two groups be educated to serve and not to lead and to reinforce society's view of their perceived natural inferiority.

This essay will focus on the attitudes of black people toward black women's education and particularly their higher education. It will also survey the purposes of education as assumed by blacks in the nineteenth century. This century served to increase educational opportunities for blacks and white women, although they remained grossly below those available to white men. Important to this essay is the impact on black women's education of the ideas of "female education" for blacks. Finally, this essay will discuss the shift in attitudes by some blacks at the turn of the century on the role of black women and the purpose of their education.

Observers of the early nineteenth century frequently cite the emergence of the notion of the ideal of "true woman" as shaping the philosophy of "female education." This concept of "true womanhood" emphasized innocence, modesty, piety, purity, submissiveness, and domesticity. "Female education" reinforced the idea of women's natural position of subordination and focused upon women's being loving wives and good mothers. Literacy for women was deemed important only for the reading of the Bible and other religious materials, and the curriculum of such education was dominated by needlepoint, painting, music, art, and French.[1]

---

[1] See, for example, Rosalind Rosenberg's *Beyond Separate Spheres: Intellectual Roots of Modern Feminism* (New Haven: Yale University Press, 1982); Nancy Cott's *The*

This model of the "ideal woman" was designed for upper-
and middle-class white women, although poor white women
often aspired to this status. This view of the fragile woman was
espoused during a period when masses of blacks were enslaved
and the debate as to whether they were human beings was a
popular topic. Thus, black women, who frequently worked
side by side with black men, were not perceived by most whites
as females as were other women in society. The lives of black
women, in and out of slavery, categorically excluded them
from such a concept.

Those members of the larger society who believed that some
type of education was necessary for blacks defined "Negro education" as being most appropriate for black women as well as
men. Since "Negro education" focused upon a belief in blacks'
intellectual and moral inferiority, such education focused on
literacy as well as on large doses of character building and
moral training. Even the more prestigious black institutions of
higher learning established by the American Missionary Association, whose curriculum included the classics, approached
their charges as persons in need of civilizing.

With the abolition of slavery in the North by the 1830s,
northern blacks immediately established independent news-
papers, schools, and other self-help organizations. Increasingly aware that many missionaries had sought only to
emancipate them, northern blacks stated they were interested
in "elevation" and not in mere emancipation. As a result, the
philosophy of "race uplift" emerged within the black community. This philosophy was the foundation of education as
viewed by blacks. This view differed dramatically from that of
their white counterparts, who stressed individual versus group

Bonds of Womanhood: "Woman's Sphere" in New England, 1780–1835 (New Haven:
Yale University Press, 1977); Sheila M. Rothman's *Woman's Proper Place: A History
of Changing Ideals and Practices, 1870 to the Present* (New York: Basic Books, 1978);
and Barbara Walter's "The Cult of True Womanhood: 1820–1860," *American Quarterly* 18 (1986): 151–174.

and male versus female achievement. Blacks, however, perceived education as a strategy for liberation and thus included
the education of women as well as men.

Repeatedly black leaders urged group solidarity and cooperation. For example, at a black national convention in 1848
Frederick Douglass impressed upon his audience its obligation
to aid members of its race still enslaved: "As one rises, all must
rise, and as one falls, all must fall. Having our feet on the rock
of freedom, we must drag our brethren from the slimy depths
of slavery, ignorance, and ruin. Every one of us should be
ashamed to consider himself free, while his brother is a slave."[2]
White observers such as John Scoble, an Englishman visiting
the United States, often commented on black group efforts. In
1835 Scoble wrote: "The free people of color, with few exceptions are true to their brethren in bonds, and are determined
to remain by them whatever the cost."[3]

In the first of many organized activities to help themselves,
free blacks in the late eighteenth century formed mutual and
benevolent societies. The African Union Society of Newport,
Rhode Island, organized in 1780 by free black men and women
"to promote the welfare of the colored community . . . by
helping apprentice Negroes, and by assisting members in the
time of distress," signaled one beginning. Similar societies,
such as the African Society of Boston and the Friendly Society
of St. Thomas in Philadelphia, also appeared in the 1790s
with the focus of their charities being the widows and orphaned
children in their communities.[4] The male African Society of
Boston expressly stated: "Should any member die, and leave a

[2] *An Address to the Colored People of the United States* in *Report of the Proceedings of
the Colored National Convention, Held at Cleveland, Ohio on Wednesday, September
6, 1848* (Rochester: 1848): 18.
[3] Quoted in Benjamin Quarles, *Black Abolitionists* (London: Oxford University Press,
1969): viii.
[4] Quoted in Irving H. Bartlett, *From Slave to Citizen: The Story of the Negro in Rhode
Island* (Providence: Urban League of Greater Providence, 1954): 35; Dorothy Porter,
ed., *Early Negro Writings, 1760–1831* (Boston: Beacon Press, 1971): 5–78.

lawful widow and children, the Society shall consider themselves bound to relieve her necessities . . . and . . . the society [shall] do the best in their power to place the children so that they may in time be capable of getting an honest living."[5] Similar organizations were founded in the South, although most functioned clandestinely.[6]

As the number of black women living in the North proliferated, they began to form separate mutual aid societies. In Philadelphia alone, by 1827, two-thirds of the 10,600 black residents of that city were female.[7] Organizations such as the Dorcas Society, the Sisterly Union, the United Daughters of Wilberforce, and the African Female Union became the means by which many black women received support during sickness or hard times. For individuals who paid 12 1/2 cents a month or $1 quarterly, a society provided assurance of a decent burial and the care of orphaned children. By 1838, of the 7,600 black members of mutual aid groups in Philadelphia, two-thirds were female. They alone raised $13,000 for their economic survival in that year in Philadelphia.[8] Black men also continued to concern themselves about the support of women and children. An 1831 advertisement in the *Philadelphia Gazette* addressed "To The Public" informed readers of many black societies formed for their mutual benefit. The advertisement stated that despite the many "privations" of people of color, it was their "duty" to lessen these through organizational means:

> The funds are exclusively appropriated to the relief of such of its members, as through sickness or misfortune, may be unable to

[5] *Laws of the African Society, Instituted at Boston 1796* (Boston: N.p., 1802).
[6] Ira Berlin, *Slaves Without Masters: The Free Negro in the Antebellum South* (New York: Vintage Books, 1974): 308–15.
[7] Edward Needles, *An Historical Memoir of the Pennsylvania Society for Promoting the Abolition of Slavery* (Philadelphia: N.p., 1848): 86.
[8] *Facts on Beneficial Societies 1823–1838 in Minutes of Pennsylvania Abolition Society,* Historical Society of Pennsylvania, Philadelphia.

work; to the interment of deceased members, and to the relief of their widows and orphans, and therefore, by contributing a trifling sum to these funds while in prosperity, we not only secure to ourselves a pension in sickness and adversity, but also contribute to the relief of our distressed brethren.[9]

Unlike white women, black women were encouraged to become educated to aid in the improvement of their race. In the New York black newspaper *The Weekly Advocate,* an 1837 article entitled "To the Females of Colour" argued that "In any enterprise for the improvement of our people, either moral or mental, our hands would be palsied without woman's influence." Thus, the article urged, "Let our beloved female friends, then rouse up, and exert all their power, in encouraging and sustaining this [educational] effort which we have made to disabuse the public mind of the misrepresentations made of our character; and to show the world, that there is virtue among us, though concealed; talent, though buried; intelligence, though overlooked."[10] In other words, black women as well as men would demonstrate the race's intelligence, morality, and ingenuity.

These views reflected not necessarily enlightenment but rather economic necessity by blacks. Throughout the nineteenth century black men were relegated to menial positions while women were primarily domestic workers. Although blacks perceived education as "uplifting," most members of society viewed the education of blacks as threatening to the white position of dominance.[11]

There were scattered opportunities for both free black and

---

[9] *Philadelphia Gazette,* March 1, 1831.

[10] *New York Weekly Advocate,* January 7, 1837.

[11] After several slave revolts by literate blacks, by emancipation every southern state had laws which prohibited the education of slaves and in many instances of free blacks as well. Carter G. Woodson, *The Education of the Negro Prior to 1861* (1919; reprint New York: Arno Press, 1968).

slaves to become literate prior to the 1830s in the nation. However, education for blacks was perceived as dangerous after the fiery *Appeal* of David Walker in 1829 and the slave revolt of Nat Turner in 1830—both literate men. After the 1830s all southern states instituted laws prohibiting the education of blacks, thus forcing such activities underground.[12]

The decades of the 1830s and 1840s, in which free blacks sought access to educational institutions in the North, paralleled the founding of seminaries for white women. Historian Anne Firor Scott points out in her study of the Troy Female Seminary, the first such institution to open, that the school combined the "true womanhood" ideal with feminist values. From its opening in 1821, under the direction of Emma Willard, the institution sought to preserve the traditional social and political status of women while challenging the notion of women's inferior intellectual status. Despite this challenge to the traditional view of the intellectual inferiority of women, Troy instilled within its students the belief that "feminine delicacy . . . was a primary and indispensable virtue."[13]

Other such seminaries proliferated in the nation prior to the Civil War. These institutions began the professional training of female teachers. However, few opened their doors to black women on a continuous basis. The lone exception was Oberlin College in Ohio, which achieved notoriety in 1833, when it decided to admit both white women and blacks on an equal basis with white men. As a result, most of the earliest black college graduates of the mid-nineteenth century, male and female, were Oberlin graduates.[14]

---

[12] Ibid.

[13] Anne Firor Scott, "The Ever Widening Circle: The Diffusion of Feminist Values from the Troy Female Seminary, 1822–1872," *History of Education Quarterly* (1979): 9.

[14] W. E. B. Du Bois, "The College Bred Negro," *Proceedings of the Fifth Conferences for the Study of the Negro Problems*, held at Atlanta University, May 29–30, 1900 (Atlanta: Atlanta University Press, 1900): 29.

Education was seen as so important for men and women that it was not atypical for black families to relocate to Oberlin for the education of their daughters. For example, when Blanche V. Harris was denied admission to a white female seminary in Michigan in the 1850s, her entire family moved to Oberlin. Similarly, Mary Jane Patterson, who in 1862 became the first black woman to earn a degree in the United States, moved from North Carolina in the 1850s to Oberlin with her family because of the educational opportunities at the college. Three Patterson females and one male graduated from Oberlin.[15] Fanny Jackson, the second black woman to earn a college degree in the nation, was sent from Washington, D.C., to Newport, Rhode Island, where her educational opportunities were greater. After completing the Rhode Island State Normal School, she also went to Oberlin and graduated in 1865. Bishop Daniel Payne of the African Methodist Episcopal Church was so impressed with Jackson's, ambition that he aided her with a scholarship to Oberlin.[16] This financial assistance is not insignificant when one remembers that when Fanny Jackson entered Oberlin in 1860, no black women in the nation had earned a college degree and very few black men had attempted higher education. Bishop Payne's enthusiasm and support for Jackson's education contrasts with the debates of the danger of higher education that surrounded the question of education for white women. These arguments stated that higher education not only reduced a woman's chance of marriage but also resulted in physical and psychological damage.[17]

As early as 1787 Benjamin Rush in his publication *Thoughts on Female Education* stated that women should be educated to become "stewards and guardians" of the family assets. And

---

[15] Ellen Henle and Marlene Merrill, "Antebellum Black Coeds at Oberlin College," *Women's Studies Newsletter* 7 (1979): 10.

[16] Ibid.

[17] Fanny Jackson Coppin, *Reminiscences of School Life and Hints on Teaching* (Philadelphia: AME Book Concern, 1913): 18.

Noah Webster warned that "education is always wrong which raises a woman above her station."[18] Even as high schools for women became available after the Civil War, the primary purposes of such institutions, according to Thomas Woody, were to extend the scope of "female education," increase the social usefulness of women, and train women as primary school teachers. For men, the high school served as preparation for college.[19]

Studies of the graduates of white female high schools and seminaries confirm that marriage usually terminated the employment of women. Teaching, the chief profession of employed, educated women, was merely a way station until matrimony. Scott's work on Troy's women students and graduates during the period 1822–1872 indicates that only 6 percent worked during marriage and only 26 percent worked at any time during their lives. David Allmendinger's research findings in his study of Mount Holyoke students during a similar period (1837–1850) are consistent with Scott's data. Although the majority of the Holyoke population taught during some point in their lives, most did so for less than five years. In addition, only 6 percent made teaching a lifetime profession.[20]

Although data on black women for these periods are inconclusive, the literature on black attitudes toward education strongly suggests that education and marriage for black women were not incompatible. W. E. B. Du Bois's study of black college graduates in 1900 indicates that 50 percent of black

[18] Benjamin Rush, *Thoughts upon Female Education, Accommodated to the Present State of Society, Manners, and Government in the United States of America* (Philadelphia: Prichard and Hall, 1787); quoted in M. A. Robinson, "The Development of Higher Education for Women in the Eastern United States, 1860–1900" (Ph.D. thesis, Oxford University, 1968).

[19] Thomas Woody, *A History of Women's Education in the United States* (New York: Science Press, 1929): 88–117.

[20] Scott, "The Ever Widening Circle": 15; David F. Allemendinger, Jr., "Mount Holyoke Students Encounter the Need for Life-Planning, 1837–1850," *History of Education Quarterly* (1979): 40.

women who had graduated between in 1860 and 1899 were married. Similarly, census statistics in 1900 reported that ten times as many married black women as married white women were employed.[21] This disproportionate ratio clearly reflects the necessity of black women to assist their families financially.

Some black women continued to work after marriage, not out of economic necessity but because of their desire to work in the interest of their race. For example, in 1884, when Fanny Jackson, principal of the prestigious Institute for Colored Youth in Philadelphia, married Levi Coppin, a prominent minister and later bishop of the African Methodist Episcopal Church, the Quaker Board of Managers of the Institute clearly anticipated her resignation and even prematurely announced her departure. However, Coppin remained as principal until her retirement in 1903. And although Mary Church Terrell, a prominent educator in Washington, D. C., was forced by law to forfeit her public school teaching post after marriage, she subsequently taught voluntarily in an evening school and became a widely known lecturer and women's club leader.[22]

Although conscious of their gender, the earliest black female graduates understood also that their desire for an education was directly linked to aiding their race. Fanny Jackson Coppin, an Oberlin graduate of 1865, wrote in her autobiography of 1913 that from girlhood her greatest ambition was "to get an education and help [her] people."[23] Anna J. Cooper, an Oberlin graduate of 1884, stated that she had decided to attend college while still in kindergarten and even then was aware of the idea of devoting her entire life to the education of her race.[24] Affluent Mary Church Terrell, also an Oberlin graduate of '84, jeopardized her inheritance when her father, who

[21] Du Bois, "The College Bred Negro": 62.
[22] 1882 *Institute for Colored Youth Annual Report.*
[23] Coppin, *Reminiscences*: 9.
[24] Negro College Graduates Questionnaire, in Anna J. Cooper Papers, Moorland-Spingarn Research Center, Howard University.

desired her to model her life on the upper-class white "true womanhood" ideal, threatened to disinherit her if she worked after graduating from Oberlin. Terrell wrote years later of this dilemma: "I had conscientiously availed myself of opportunities for preparing myself for a life of usefulness as only four other colored [women] had been able to do. . . . All during my college course I had dreamed of the day when I could promote the welfare of my race."[25]

During the antebellum era "race uplift" was the expected objective of *all* blacks. However, after the Civil War the implementation of this philosophy was increasingly placed on the shoulders of black women. Of the many blacks who migrated or returned South after emancipation to aid in the transition from slavery to freedom, prominent among them were women. For example, Louise De Montie, a noted lecturer who had migrated from Virginia to Boston in the 1850s, moved to New Orleans in 1865 to open the city's first orphanage for black youth. Mary Shadd Cary, who had migrated to Canada in the late 1850s, returned to the United States after the outbreak of the war to serve as a scout for the Union army. Scores of other black women went South to engage in the massive effort to educate the newly emancipated blacks.[26]

Throughout the war and afterward, northern black women raised money and collected clothes to send South. On one occasion the Colored Ladies Sanitary Commission of Boston sent $500 to blacks in Savannah. Similarly, in Washington, D.C., Elizabeth Keckley, the mulatto seamstress of First Lady Mary Lincoln, organized with forty other black women the

[25] Mary Church Terrell, *A Colored Woman in a White World* (Washington, D.C.: National Association of Colored Women's Clubs, 1968): 59–60.
[26] Martin Delany to Mary Shadd Cary, December 7, 1853, biographical folder, Mary Shadd Cary Papers, Moorland-Spingarn Research Center, Howard University; John W. Blassingame, *Black New Orleans, 1860–80* (Chicago: University of Chicago Press, 1973): 170; George Washington Williams, *A History of the Negro Race in America* (New York: Bergman Publishers, 1883): 2:449.

Contraband Relief Association of Washington in 1862. In its first two years of existence the group sent nearly one hundred boxes and barrels of clothing to southern blacks and spent in excess of $1,600.[27]

Perhaps more impressive were the efforts of black women in the South to aid themselves. Viewing charity primarily as an activity of the fortunate to aid the unfortunate, white missionaries frequently recorded with astonishment the establishment of black self-help groups. One such report cited a group of poor black women in Charleston, South Carolina, who formed an organization to aid the sick. After working all day, members of the group devoted several hours to duty in the hospitals.[28] *The National Freedmen*, the publication of the National Freedom Relief Society, often reported the generous charity among blacks in general and black women in particular. One such missionary report stated: "I have been greatly struck with the charity of these colored people. There are few of them even comfortably situated for this world's goods. Yet, their charity is the most extensive, hearty, genuine thing imaginable. They have innumerable organizations for the relief of the aged, the helpless or needy from whatever."[29] The observer was greatly impressed by the work of black women. He wrote that he witnessed black women "past the prime of life and with no visible means of support" who took in whole families of orphaned children.[30] Although these stories are chronicled with repeated surprise in missionary letters, similar stories are found with regularity in slave testimonies, and such actions were viewed not as unique but rather as routine within the black community.

Despite the significant contributions of black women to the

---

[27] James M. McPherson, *The Negro's Civil War: How American Negroes Felt and Acted During the War for the Union* (New York: Vintage Books, 1965): 136–38.
[28] Ibid.
[29] *The National Freedmen* (May 1, 1865).
[30] Ibid.

economic, civic, religious, and educational improvement of the race, after emancipation there was a noticeable shift in the attitudes toward the role of women by many members of the race. Several reasons explain this shift in attitude. First, the passage in 1870 of the Fifteenth Amendment, granting blacks the franchise, signaled the first major gender distinction made among blacks by American society. By 1900 twenty-two black men had served in the nation's Congress and scores of others held state and local government posts.[31] These accomplishments and opportunities for black men to exert authority and power, even though only for a brief moment, dramatically altered the view that many had toward the role of women. This change in attitude was manifested in a variety of ways.

For example, by the 1880s articles within the black press had begun expressing a conservative view of women reminiscent of those written in antebellum New England. Unlike articles prior to the Civil War which urged black women to join with black men in obtaining an education, black publications frequently indicated that the black woman's place was in the home. Further, these articles stated that education for black women should be moral education primarily as preparation for motherhood and marriage. Articles entitled "Shall Our Girls Be Educated?," "The Homemaker," and "Woman's Exalted Station," which appeared in the 1880s and 1890s in the *AME Review*, a popular journal published by the African Methodist Episcopal Church, glorified homemaking and encouraged the education of women to "prepare their sons for manhood."[32] Second, this shift in attitudes by some men of the race was a result of their acculturation of mainstream values and norms. It was indeed a patriarchal society, and blacks were attempting to "uplift" themselves to the standards of the majority culture. Historian Joel Williamson, in assessing black male attitudes

[31] John Hope Franklin, *From Slavery to Freedom*, 3d ed. (New York: Vintage Books, 1969): 317–20.
[32] *AME Review* (1889): 45–47; 8 (1891): 63–65; 8 (1892): 402–06.

toward women after emancipation, noted that most black men "internalized fully the role of Victorian men."[33] Although Victorian gender roles may have been desired by some black males, in reality they were not economically able to sustain a patriarchal existence. Married black women had to work, and a disproportionate number of black women in the North were single. Thus, education and economic survival for black women became paramount issues for black female leadership.

Oberlin College produced a small cadre of articulate, classically trained, race-conscious, and feminist black women during the nineteenth century. Prominent among them were Fanny Jackson Coppin, '65, principal of the prestigious Institute for Colored Youth in Philadelphia; Anna Julia Cooper, '84, former teacher of M Street School, the well-known black public high school in Washington, D.C.; and Mary Church Terrell, '84, former teacher of M Street School, member of the District of Columbia School Board, and noted clubwoman. These women, along with a growing number of other college-trained black women, took active leadership roles within their local communities and were known nationally. For these women, a desire to "uplift" their race was a primary motivation for obtaining a college degree.[34]

Black women leaders were particularly active in the 1890s and placed increased emphasis on issues related to women. Although interested in the status of the race as a whole, the small number of college-trained black women were aware of the increased opportunities opening for white women and of the strides black men had made during Reconstruction. The status of black women, however, remained virtually unchanged throughout the century. By 1890 only 30 black women had

[33] Joel Williamson, *New People: Miscegenation and Mulattoes in the United States* (New York: Free Press, 1980): 91.
[34] See Coppin, *Reminiscences*; Anna Julia Cooper's biographical folder, Anna J. Cooper Papers, Spingarn Research Center, Howard University; and Terrell, *Colored Woman in a White World*.

earned baccalaureate degrees, compared with more than 300 black men and 2,500 white women. [35]

Although most nineteenth-century educated black women believed women morally superior to men, few believed that women should be subordinate to men or should limit their activities to the domestic domain. Considering the complete disfranchisement of southern blacks during the final decades of the century, the lynching of black men, and the sexual assaults of white men on southern black women, sexism was a luxury blacks could not afford.

As early as 1878 Fanny Jackson Coppin started a newspaper column in the *Christian Recorder*, the newspaper of the AME Church, to give educational and career advice to black women. By the 1890s black women in urban areas throughout the nation sought to assist unemployed women of the race. Mary Church Terrell reported in 1894 on the serious labor problem of black women in Washington, D.C., and noted that the Colored Women's League, established in 1892, was seeking to aid them. It did not go unnoticed by black women leaders that white women were making great strides in education and employment by the 1890s. More than 100,000 white women were employed as salesclerks by 1890. And by the turn of the century more than half of all business school students were women. Even in the South, as historian Anne Firor Scott reports, by 1900 large numbers of single white women of all classes were employed. Yet the 1900 census reported that 96 percent of black women workers were employed as either domestics or agricultural workers. [36]

[35] Frank Bowles and Frank A. DeCosta, *Between Two Worlds: A Profile of Negro Higher Education* (New York: McGraw-Hill, 1971): 13.

[36] *Christian Recorder*, June 27, 1878, and July 25, 1878; *The Woman's Era* (December 1894); Barbara Mayer Wertheimer, *We Were There: The Story of Working Women in America* (New York: Pantheon Books, 1977): 159; Anne Firor Scott, *The Southern Lady: From Pedestal to Politics, 1830–1930* (Chicago: University of Chicago Press, 1970): 129.

In 1892 Anna J. Cooper addressed the issue of sexism in *A Voice from the South*. She noted the paucity of black women who had obtained a higher education and placed the blame squarely upon the lack of encouragement from black men. Cooper wrote, "I fear the majority of colored men do not yet think it worthwhile that women aspire to higher education. . . . Let money be raised and scholarships be founded in our colleges and universities for self-supporting worthy young women." Consistent with the thinking of the era, Cooper argued that educated women made better mothers and wives. Thus, women should not fear that classical education would impede their chances for marriage. And black men should understand that her advocacy of greater opportunities for black women should not be interpreted as less for men, simply more for women.[37] Unfortunately, however, for many in the race more education for black women *was* perceived as less for black men.

By the end of the century higher education and leadership went hand in hand in the black community. The nation was becoming increasingly industrial, new fields of inquiry such as sociology and anthropology were emerging, and many of the attacks upon the intellectual capabilities of blacks that emerged were the results of "scientific" studies. Therefore, it became necessary for blacks to counterattack these studies with their own and produce their own intelligentsia. This philosophy was shared by many blacks, male and female, but was articulated most forcefully by W. E. B. Du Bois. Believing that education should serve to "uplift" blacks, Du Bois espoused the notion of the "talented tenth," the educated black elite. This philosophy collided with that of Booker T. Washington, who was thrust into the limelight after his infamous Atlanta address of 1895, in which he advocated an accommodationist stance for blacks in race relations and urged industrial education.[38]

---

[37] Cooper, A *Voice from the South*: 75, 79.
[38] For more on Washington, see Louis Harlan, *Booker T. Washington: The Making*

The debate between Du Bois and Washington concerning classical versus industrial education is well known and has been widely discussed in many scholarly works. The critical questions concerning black education, as Du Bois noted in 1903, was not whether "men should be carpenters, but whether carpenters should be men."[39] Thus, the fundamental issue was whether education should prepare blacks to challenge or accommodate the status quo. Black women leaders generally agreed with Du Bois and, in fact, encouraged black women to campaign for suffrage as well as to pursue a higher education.

With black women increasingly concerned about the special plight of black girls and the large population of single black women, numerous attempts were made to establish schools exclusively for black females. This was a radical departure from the practice of nineteenth-century blacks, who had established schools without regard for gender. Although single sex institutions of education existed for blacks, without exception, they had normally been founded by whites. Spelman College in Atlanta, Georgia, for example, was established by two white New England women in 1881.[40] After 1900 the move to found schools for only black women was prompted primarily by black women who believed that they had not reaped sufficient benefits in education or employment during Reconstruction. To be sure, the turn of the century was indeed the nadir for most blacks since for a brief period during Reconstruction black men had moved into leadership roles and advanced educationally.

---

of a Black Leader, 1856–1901 (New York: Oxford University Press, 1971); and Hugh Hawkins, ed., *Booker T. Washington and the Negro's Place In American Life* (Boston: Little, Brown, 1955).

[39] W. E. B. Du Bois, "The Talented Tenth," in Booker T. Washington et al., *The Negro Problem: A Series of Articles by Representative American Negroes of To-day* (1903; New York: Arno Press, 1969): 63.

[40] Bennett College, established in 1873 by the Methodist Episcopal Church as a coeducational institution, became a women's college in 1926. Beverly Guy-Sheftall, "Black Women and Higher Education: Spelan and Bennett Colleges Revisited," *Journal of Negro Education* 51 (1982): 278–87.

More significantly, however, numerous influential black males discouraged the gender-egalitarian notions prevalent among blacks in the earlier decades of the nineteenth century. For example, the American Negro Academy, the first black learned society, founded in 1897, constitutionally prohibited women. From its establishment until its dissolution in 1928, the organization listed as members the most prominent and active black men of the nation. The group produced twenty-two occasional papers which addressed an array of issues concerning race and race relations. None, however, addressed concerns relating to black women.[41]

By the turn of the century a decided shift in focus for black women educators can be noted. Lucy Laney, a black educator from Augusta, Georgia, addressed the Hampton Negro Conference in 1899 and spoke of the particular plight of black women. Laney was born free in Georgia in 1854 and had attended the schools of the American Missionary Association. In 1863 she graduated from the first normal class of Atlanta University. In 1866, with the assistance of the Presbyterian Board of Missions, Laney founded the Haines Normal and Industrial Institute in Augusta, Georgia. Addressing the 1899 conference, Laney spoke of the "burden of the educated Negro

---

[41] A recent biography of Anna J. Cooper states that she was the only woman member of the organization. Louise Daniel Hutchinson, *Anna J. Cooper: A Voice from the South* (Washington, D.C.: Smithsonian Institution Press, 1981): 109. This assertion conflicts with that of a history of the American Negro Academy. According to Alfred Moss, Jr., women were barred from the organization. Moss writes: "When in December, 1897, Anna J. Cooper, a prominent member of Washington's black intellectual elite, wrote an article on the academy for the *Southern Workman*, it was her understanding that its membership was 'confined to men.' " Moss also notes: "Although the black community produced some outstanding female artists, educators, and civic leaders during the late nineteenth and early twentieth centuries—figures such as Fanny Jackson Coppin, Ida Wells-Barnett, Mary Church Terrell, Lucy Laney, Nannie Burroughs, Meta Warrick Fuller, and Alice Dunbar-Nelson—nothing was done to draw them into a relationship with the American Negro Academy." Alfred A. Moss, Jr., *The American Negro Academy: Voice of the Talented Tenth* (Baton Rouge: Louisiana State University Press, 1899).

woman." Although the "burden" was great, educated black women were necessary for the "uplifting" of the race. Although such women were needed as teachers of small children, Laney added that black women were needed as teachers of *all* levels, including high school, the academy, and college. Furthermore, educated black women were necessary as public lecturers in the community as well as in the classroom. In closing, Laney emphasized that blacks needed the talents not only of men as leaders but women as well.[42] This message was to be repeated by other educated black women for decades to come.

Lucy Laney had, in fact, intended the Haines Institute to be a school only for women. However, the educational needs of both sexes won out in the end. Although Haines suffered from financial problems, it prospered and developed an outstanding academic reputation. In 1931 the school had enrolled 300 students and employed 27 teachers. With Laney's death in 1933 and the Great Depression, the school declined. It officially closed its doors in 1949.[43]

Mary McLeod Bethune, who became a renowned educator and international figure, was inspired by Lucy Laney to establish a school for black girls. Bethune taught at the Haines Institute for one year and later moved to Daytona Beach, Florida, where she opened the Daytona Normal and Industrial School for Negro Girls in 1904. Believing that racial inequality would not be eradicated until black girls obtained the same educational opportunities available to white girls, Bethune devoted her entire life to improving the lives of black youth and black women. The school merged with a male institution and became Bethune-Cookman College in 1923. In the tradition of Booker T. Washington, Bethune stressed teacher, religious, and vocational education.[44]

[42] Lucy Laney, "The Burden of the Educated Colored Woman," in *Hampton Negro Conference* 3 (Hampton, Va.: Hampton Institute Press, 1899).
[43] "Lucy Laney," in *Dictionary of American Negro Biography*, ed. Rayford W. Logan and Michael R. Winston (New York: W. W. Norton): 380.
[44] See Catherine Owens Peare, *Mary McLeod Bethune* (New York: Vanguard Press,

Linda M. Perkins

With the shifting attitudes toward women within the black
community at the century's end, educated black women focused
their attention primarily on youth and women. Because such
interests were viewed as appropriately women's concerns, black
women who sought roles outside their expected spheres suffered pain, rejection, and ridicule. Such traditional and conservative views of women were held by blacks across class and
educational lines. For example, after the wealthy Mary Church
Terrell graduated from Oberlin College in 1884, she was dis-
inherited by her father when she decided to work. She stated:
"It was held by most people that women were unfitted to do
their work in the home if they studied Latin, Greek, and higher
mathematics. . . . I was ridiculed and told that no man would
want to marry a woman who studied higher mathematics."[45]
Those black women born during the latter decades of the nineteenth century perhaps experienced the greatest conflict between
the needs of the race and society's view of a woman's role. Oral
histories of black women who grew up during this period paint
a vivid picture of the dilemma of black women seeking to "uplift"
the race as well as be "true women."

Dr. May Edward Chinn, born in 1896, was the only woman
doctor in Harlem for fifty years. She recalled that her father
was deeply embarrassed by her educational pursuits and not

1951); Rackham Holt, *Mary McLeod Bethune : A Biography* (New York: Doubleday,
1964). Another pioneer was Nannie Burroughs, a graduate of M Street High School
in Washington, D.C., who founded the National Training School for Women and
Girls in 1909 in Washington. Burroughs was a prominent churchwoman in the Baptist Church, and her school was initially funded by the women of the National Baptist
Woman's Convention, an auxiliary to the men's convention. The school's purposes
were to prepare black girls for homemaking, respectable careers, and the development
of "Christian womanhood." Sewing, home economics, practical and home nursing,
bookkeeping, shorthand, typing, gardening, laundering, interior design, printing, shoe
repairing, and barbering were taught. The school closed after Burroughs's death in
1961. Evelyn Brooks Barnett, "Nannie Burroughs and the Education of Black Women,"
in *The Afro-American Woman: Struggles and Images*, ed. Sharon Harley and Rosalyn
Terborg-Penn (Fort Washington, N.Y.: Kennikat Press, 1978): 97–108; "Mary McLeod
Bethune," in *Dictionary of American Negro Biography*: 41–43.
[45] Quoted in Jeanne Noble, *The Negro Women's College Education* : (New York: Bureau
of Publications, Teachers College, Columbia University, 1956): 23.

only discouraged her but provided no financial support. Chinn's mother was a domestic who often lived in with white families. Her father did odd jobs when he could find employment but was frequently unemployed. Despite the fact that her mother provided the steady income to the family and encouraged her education, Chinn's father believed a woman's role was in the home. Chinn recollected: "My father objected to me going to college, number one. . . . His idea of a girl was that you got married and had children. He was of a different generation. A girl that went to college became a queer woman. And he did not want to be the father of a queer girl."[46] Although Chinn never married, one of her contemporaries, Dorothy Spaulding Ferebee, M.D., did. Born in 1898, she graduated from the Tufts University School of Medicine and became a faculty member of Freedmen's Hospital of Howard University in the late 1920s. Ferebee married a dentist in 1930 and said that professional jealousy ended the relationship within a few years. She stated: "You see, he [her husband] was becoming more and more resentful of everything that I was doing as a woman, because what I attempted seemed to turn to gold, and his effort was turning to mud, you understand. After the first year or so, I knew what was on his mind. The fact that I became busier and had perhaps a larger group of patients, that didn't settle too well with him. And for that reason, he became very, shall I say, not disgruntled, but unhappy and uncooperative, and insisted that I give up my work. Of course, I wasn't going to do that[47] Ferebee immersed herself in the black community. She became medical director of Howard University Health Services and medical director of the Mississippi Health Proj-

[46] Interview, May Edward Chinn, June 27, July 13, and September 12, 1979. Black Women's Oral History Project, Schlesinger Library, Radcliffe College, Cambridge, Mass.: 23.
[47] Interview, Dorothy Spaulding Ferebee, December 28 and 31, 1979, Black Women's Oral History Project, Schlesinger Library, Radcliffe College, Cambridge, Mass.: 14.

ect, a project to aid tenant farming families in two Mississippi counties. As did many educated black women of her generation, Ferebee sought to "uplift" the race and particularly black women. She became the second president of the National Council of Negro Women, succeeding the founder, Mary McLeod Bethune, and the head of Alpha Kappa Alpha Sorority, and she served on the national boards of the Girl Scouts of America and the YWCA and numerous other organizations.[48] Although other educated black women of Chinn and Ferebee's generation experienced similar difficulties, many did state that they received encouragement and support from fathers, uncles, and husbands.

Little is known of the "burden," as Lucy Laney termed it, of the educated black women. Until recently the twentieth century has been silent on most aspects of black women's education except for the writings of such black women educators as Lucy Slowe, Marion Cuthbert, Willa Player, and Jeanne Noble. Most nineteenth-century educated black women sought to "uplift" the race through educational, religious, and civic endeavors. By the century's end the notion of a "woman's sphere" clashed with that of "race uplift," thus resulting in most "uplift" activities being done in women's organizations.

Much more research remains to be done on the complexity of gender roles and perceptions of gender roles historically within the black community. As noted above, the oppression and discrimination experienced by all blacks resulted in traditional gender roles being blurred for most of the nineteenth century. This oppression of all blacks, ironically, resulted in a more egalitarian attitude toward women by most blacks up until the end of the nineteenth century. As race "progress" (i.e., educational and economic gains) was made, patriarchy became a major ingredient in this notion. This is understandable, indeed, since in the larger society men were the leaders, thinkers, and

[48] Ibid.

financial supporters of their families. Anything less resulted in a man's not being considered a "real" man. While it is true that black men have historically been denied the opportunity to participate fully as equals with whites in American society, the same can be said of black women.

The issue of sexism within the black community remains an issue that requires much more exploration. This form of discrimination, like racism, unfortunately resulted in many talented individuals' not being able to live up to their greatest potentials.

JEANNE NOBLE
The Higher Education of Black Women in the Twentieth Century

A distinguishing fact about black women's pursuit of higher education during the first half of this century was their sense of mission. Certainly they were motivated by the practical necessity to prepare for jobs that would enable them to earn decent livings, but this need was matched by a commitment to achieve goals of "race uplift" that would eventually lead black people from legal discrimination and segregation to freedom. These early generations had a strong "historic memory" of black people's plight and the racial obligations to be shouldered as college-educated blacks.[1] They believed what Booker T. Washington taught: "Lift As You Climb."

[1] Linda Perkins, "The Impact of the Cult of True Womanhood on the Education of Black Women," *Journal of Social Issues* 29 (November 3, 1983):16–26. "Historic memory" is used here to describe a conscious memory of collective history, literature,

---

JEANNE NOBLE *is professor of education at Brooklyn College, the City University of New York, Brooklyn.*

There is concern that today's black students may well be a generation with neither historic memory nor altruistic motivation to help achieve black group goals. This apparent lack of "mission motivation" among the current generation of black college students may well be consistent with the self-serving values shared by many college students, white or black. Many social commentators believe that this current generation of college students lacks idealism and is preoccupied with pursuing affluence and material riches. All of society suffers when egocentric attitudes diminish civic values. More specifically, however, blacks, only a quarter century removed from legal segregation and still living in a racist society, desperately need commitment and leadership skills from each successive generation. When significant numbers of educated youth become indifferent to a mission of "race uplift," the gains made by previous generations are jeopardized. There is a continuing need for strong, educated black leadership to advance the interests of black people.

art, music, and traditions—all that tells the story of a people: how they came to be, how they suffered and triumphed, what strategies of survival and success worked in the past, and what the obstacles seem to be for future progress. This memory is not passive but actively operates in a person so that she engages in activities that keep the memories alive and passes them along to the next generation and the next. A scriptural reference expresses the meaning more eloquently (Deut. 32:7): "Remember the days of old, consider the ages past, ask your father (mother), he (she) will inform you, your elders will tell you." Freud acknowledged his membership in "his fated people's past" as an essential component in the development of the human psyche. Efforts to ignore a group kinship and the overidealize the dominant group's history and values were labeled "self-hatred" by Kurt Lewin. Erik Erikson suggested that an integration of one's cultural identity with a personal identity was necessary in establishing a healthy identity. All of human history, from the Jewish-German experience to Lech Walesa's Solidarity struggle in Poland, teaches us that freedom once denied and won in struggle is never secure. Each surviving generation has to regain and reclaim ground and will struggle for freedom again and again. This quest for freedom begins in the minds of young students. A generation without a historic memory is one that has little or no connection with, identification with, or appreciation of its people's past, no identity with its people's history. The majority group's ideals, goals, and values have become internalized and demand nearly all their energies and concerns.

8 8

The "missing motivation" expressed by so many black women in the early twentieth century was related to certain problems in black education. Measured by the standards governing white colleges, the faculties at black colleges were generally inadequate. The 46,950 teachers, slightly more than 1,000 of them college teachers, were overwhelmed by 5 million students. The lack of competent black teachers was the most critical issue.[2]

It was an emphasis on a teaching mission, then, that led many black women to seek admission to the seventeen black land-grant colleges, even though they lacked high school certificates. In 1928, 14,028 black students were admitted to college by high school certificate, 64 percent of them women; 73 percent of those admitted by examination were women. Black women seemed to be highly motivated to achieve college educations and become teachers. The enrollment of black women exceeded that of males in both the first and second years of college. By the third and fourth years the attraction of teaching with a credential of a two-year certificate resulted in more black men's remaining to complete the college curriculum.

Black women numbered only 22 of the 156 graduates of black colleges in 1900, but by 1910 women slightly outnumbered black male college graduates. With the exception of the decade between 1920 and 1930, black women have earned more college degrees than black men in this century. This is an important distinguishing factor of higher education for blacks during the first fifty years of the century and in direct contrast with the white college population.[3]

Many black women who went to college to become teachers were inspired with an altruistic mission to teach an over-

[2] Ambrose A. Caliver, "Background Study of Negro College Students," *Office of Education Bulletin*, No. 8 (Washington, D.C.: Government Printing Office, 1933); Dwight O. W. Holmes, *The Evolution of the Negro-College* (New York: Teachers College, Columbia University, 1934).
[3] Jeanne Noble, *The Negro College Woman's College Education* (New York: Teachers College, Columbia University, 1956). Hereafter Noble (1956).

whelming number of unschooled children. Having observed the New England schoolmarms, those white missionary women who went south after the Civil War to teach the freedom, many families had already seen role models for their daughters and granddaughters to emulate. Teaching was an acceptable feminine occupation. A young woman could achieve an esteemed social standing, improve her economic condition, and avoid working in a white home as a domestic servant. She could escape the daily, often humiliating contact with white people. Holding an acceptable and admired position among her people often compensated for the degradation of segregation.[4]

Filling the crying need for teachers may have been one most urgent motivation for women seeking a college education, but training in home economics was a close second in the minds of leaders of the black community. In fact, black collegiate programs in home economics for women developed more rapidly and consistently than did agriculture and mechanical arts for men. Black women studied nutrition, tailoring, home management, invalid care, laundering, and other domestic subjects. During the first half of the century many of these students were interested in becoming home demonstration agents. This job entailed home visitations to isolated rural areas for the purposes of teaching home and child care. Even though the need for this service was important to blacks, this heavy emphasis on a home economics curriculum, often at the expense of an adequate academic program, might well have been influenced by whites, who needed adequately trained domestic help in their homes and institutions. Black women had only a few occupations available to them. They could teach, they could become home demonstration agents, or they could end up as cooks or cleaning women in white homes.

Black women may have outnumbered black men in the col-

---

[4] Jeanne Noble, *Beautiful, Also, Are the Souls of My Black Sisters* (Englewood Cliffs, N.J.: Prentice-Hall, 1979). Hereafter Noble (1979).

lege population, but they were not in major decision-making positions; black men controlled black institutions. While the black community encouraged black women to seek and education "for the good of the race," black male educational leaders tempered their acceptance of educated women by advocating that their education be "different." Major curriculum recommendations centered on moral and Christian education. While moral education was a common concern in the higher education of all women, black men appeared especially sensitive about the sexual abuse of black women by white men during slavery and Reconstruction. Abhorrence of concubinage relationships between white men and black women influenced the thinking of those adamant about protecting future generations of black women from their so-called baser instincts. Unresolved feelings about the black woman's sexual role in the white world, as expressed by some of the male educators, seemed to raise the question, Did black women encourage and enjoy sexual liaisons with white men? Precautions against future generations of black women's being so tempted were introduced into the college environment. "Race uplift" took on an additional obligation for black college women; they were to advance the educational goals of the race by teaching the young and also "lift up" the moral character of the race by demonstrating sexual virtue. [5]

Black male educators were also influenced by the arguments and debates among whites concerning women's inherent ability to be educated or to study certain subjects. The respected black scholar and leader Kelly Miller, dean of Howard University, publicly expressed sympathy for the view that women were incapable of higher education. Miller not only

---

[5] Kelly Miller, *Race and Adjustment* (New York: Neale Publishing Company, 1909); Alexander Crummel, *Africa and America* (Springfield, Mass.: Wiley & Company, 1891); Thomas Nelson Baker, "The Negro Woman," *Alexander's Magazine* 2 (December 15, 1906); Jack Thorne, *A Plea for Social Justice for the Negro Woman* (Yonkers, N. Y.: Lincoln Press Association, 1912).

fought against women's suffrage but argued that the female sex was inherently weak.[6]

Other black men might well have been more vocal in espousing Miller's sexism but for the need for teachers. Many black men were torn between the need for teachers and a desire to emulate the white ideal of the "cult of true womanhood." The desire both to train teachers and to develop morally virtuous women led to an amalgamation of these philosophies. In 1906 Thomas Baker summarized the attitudes of most leading male educators toward the education of black women: "She must not be educated away from being a mother; slave days degraded motherhood and made merchandise out of it. The race is dependent on her giving her best to her children. . . . She needs, for the sake of the race to be better educated than them [sic]. Mothers of men should be superior in order to rear superior men. . . . Her education should be rooted in Christian education." This "better education" did not mean more formal education than that of black men; it meant a highly moral education with emphasis on proper sexual mores.[7]

These prevailing attitudes led to very stringent rules governing the conduct of black women students. Some educators, particularly W. E. B. Du Bois, considered the environment for black male and female students oppressive and cautioned that "prisonlike discipline" interfered with the development of intellectual faculties. Nevertheless, black women were more rigidly overprotected by rules and regulations governing their moral behavior than were black men or white women. Chapel and Bible classes were included as college requirements.[8]

One of the acknowledged leaders of higher education for black women, Lucy Slowe, dean of women at Howard Uni-

[6] Kelly Miller, "Women's Suffrage," *The Crisis* II (November 1915): 7–8; Perkins, "Impact of the Cult of True Womanhood."
[7] Lucy Slowe, "Higher Education for Negro Women," *Journal of Negro Education* 2 (July 1933): 352–358.
[8] Ibid.

versity, rebelled against the emphasis on moral education, with its attention to women's sexual behavior and focused instead on the kind of education black women needed in order to function adequately and realistically in their communities. According to Slowe, if black women "are to be intelligent members of their communities, more of them must pursue those subjects which have to do with community life. The classical courses must be supplemented by the Social Sciences which enable one to understand the world in which one lives. . . . Whether or not Negro college women will be able to take their place as leaders in their communities depends on the opportunities offered them for exercising initiative, independence, and self-direction while in college."

Slowe's 1933 study of black women college students pointed out that fewer than 50 percent of the colleges actually gave women opportunities for self-government or self-direction. Since black coeds came from communities where they were denied the vote and lived in poor homes where fundamentalist religion preached an inferior status of women, she believed black colleges must help black women develop a positive self-direction:

> The belief exists that college women must be shielded and protected to such an extent that the most intimate phases of their lives are invaded by rules and regulations. . . . College women must be trained along the line of their individual talents and at the same time they must be conscious of the fact that the world will expect from them practically the same sort of contribution of an individual so disciplined that she can direct herself and so informed that she can assist in directing others in this intricate modern world. Institutions of higher learning must furnish the world this type of individual.

Clearly, Dean Slowe espoused a very different education for black women from that which the men had advocated.

Her philosophy was in the best tradition of a "mission educa-tion."[9]

In 1942, eight years after Dean Slowe's study, Marion Cuthbert published the first scholarly book about the educa-tion of black women. Greatly influenced by Lucy Slowe's work, Cuthbert described the many expectations society held for black college women as well as black women's own concerns about their roles and functions. She raised many important ques-tions: How useful was a college education to the individual woman? How useful was her education to the masses of oppressed blacks? What problems did women college gradu-ates face? What were their hopes and dreams for themselves as college-educated citizens? According to Cuthbert, black women were influenced to seek a college education by the need for teachers in the black community, by the need for additional income to assist in family support, by the availability of women for schooling since they could be spared from farm work, by the prestige associated with sending a girl to college so that she might return home and introduce the family to new ways, and by the opportunity for her to meet a young man and marry well, thereby elevating her social status. In short, while "mis-sion motivation" continued to be an important consideration for these women, their personal adjustment to life after college overshadowed racial goals.[10]

Cuthbert concluded that the primary source of tension among black college women was their marginal status in society. Caught up in a "marginality syndrome," they expressed feelings of iso-lation and estrangement from any significant social reference group. Unaccepted by both black men and white college men and women, they fell adrift, not fully at home anywhere. Fur-thermore, a college education created social distance between themselves and their uneducated families. Finally, failure to

[9] Ibid.
[10] Marion Vera Cuthbert, *Education and Marginality* (New York: Stratford Press, 1942).

find ideal college-educated husbands contributed further to their personal and social maladjustments.

Cuthbert's study influenced three other studies that further explored black women's expectations of a college education and how prepared they were for their marginal status as college-educated women. While each of these studies advanced the belief that black women needed to be prepared for "race uplift" participation, a utilitarian need for education which prepared a woman for a variety of roles was the major focus of all three. Ina Bolton investigated the extent to which several black colleges assisted women in solving several major life problems. She found a disparity between what the colleges offered and what the woman needed as preparation for life experiences. Bolton concluded that black colleges should offer more courses and counseling in self-understanding, marriage and family life, career development, and social skills.[11]

Willa Player, the first black woman college president since Mary McLeod Bethune, produced a doctoral study that led to the revision of the curriculum of Bennett College. This was the first study of black college's alumnae that attempted to evaluate the influence of the college's curriculum and environment in the lives of its graduates. Player was very much influenced by the Sarah Lawrence curriculum and its president, Harold Taylor, a leading exponent of the instrumentalist philosophy of education. This philosophy advocated a college curriculum devoted to helping each individual develop all her personal powers so that she learned to satisfy her own needs and shared in caring for the needs of contemporary society. While this philosophy was closely related to a philosophy of individualism, both Taylor, and later Player, in redesigning Bennett College's curriculum, believed that the fulfillment of

---

[11] Ina Bolton, "Problems of Negro College Women Graduates" (E.D. diss., University of California, 1948).

individual needs was best achieved in a moral contest requiring the individual to give part of herself to others.[12]

In 1956, when I published my study of black women graduates, "mission motivation" or "race uplift" themes in education had become part of the need for a broad utilitarian education that considered the life-situational needs of black women as equally important. The majority of the women in this study worked actively in their communities and believed their college educations should prepare them for such service. They were sensitive to the plight of their race. Yet clearly there were expectations that their own needs, particularly the need to get a good job, would be met. A strong utilitarian drive to gain a college education in order to get a good job was evident. Other educational goals, such as education for personal development, international understanding, the pursuit of learning for learning's sake, or the expansion of one's mind, were respected, but they appeared more a luxury than a necessity. In many ways these women, more than thirty years ago, were like the present generation of college students, black and white, who think that college should, above all else, train them for a career.[13]

This utilitarian theme was understandable in view of the economic plight of blacks. Black women realized the need for their paychecks in order to sustain decent standards of living. Yet the rejection of educational goals which develop a liberated mind and enhance self-actualization made this population of black women different from white college women of their generation. Many studies of that time described white college women as being primarily interested in education for self-fulfillment and in the goal of learning to be personally

[12] Willa Player, "Improving College Education for Women at Bennett College" (Doctor of Education project, Teachers College, Columbia University, 1948); Harold Taylor, "The Philosophical Foundation of General Education," in *Yearbook of the National Society for the Study of Education*, ed. Nelson Henry (Chicago: University of Chicago Press, 1952).
[13] Noble (1956).

interesting and enlightened. Black women found training for an occupation and citizenship education more important than whites did. Black women also gave considerably more importance to training for marriage and family life than did white women.[14]

The practical necessities of life seemed to overwhelm more spiritual self-fulfillment needs or values for black women. Yet while economic realism was an important concern, women expressed the view that college should be more than mere vocational training. In the 1950s I wrote:

> The respondents thought least important, (1) development of a good moral character; (2) education for international understanding and cooperation, and (3) a better appreciation of such things as art, music, and literature. Even the item "the intelligence and wisdom to live a full life" was chosen by less than half of the respondents as most important.
>
> The subordination of these aspects raises a serious question as to whether these women lack confidence in their right to seek self-fulfillment. Does the hard earthy need for holding a job and contributing to the family budget mean that learning for full, creative living must be relegated to a lesser sphere? Maybe to these women, the concept of self-fulfillment seems a luxury. Yet it appears that the more doggedly they see themselves as breadwinners, so to speak, rather than as women who have a right to develop their personal interests and abilities, the more urgent is the need to encourage them to develop themselves as persons. Under the stark and grim

[14] Elmo Roper, "The Public Look at Higher Education," *Fortune* (September 1949); Jane B. Berry, "Life Plans of Freshmen and Sophomore Women" (Doctor of Education project, Teachers College, Columbia University, 1954); Robert Shosteck, *Five Thousand College Women Report* (Washington, D.C.: B'nai B'rith Vocational Service Bureau, 1953); American Association of University Women, *AAUW Women Look at College Education: An Interim Report* (Washington, D.C.: The Association, 1944); Grace Foster, *Social Change in Relation to Curriculum Development in Collegiate Education for Women* (Waterville, Maine: Galahead Press, 1934); Pauline P. Wilson, *College Women Who Express Futility* (New York: Teachers College, Columbia University, 1950).

necessities of life that they point out, there is something poignant about what they did not choose.

In the 1970s, when I wrote *Beautiful, Also, Are the Souls of My Black Sisters,* an emphasis on economic security was still pronounced among black women. It doubtlessly continues today as the chief motivation for getting a college education.[15]

The black revolution of the 1960s marked a monumental step forward for blacks. Furthermore, the Economic Opportunity Act of 1964 and the Education Act of 1965 created new educational opportunities for blacks. One of the earliest benefits of this legislation was the rapid entrance of black students into previously segregated white colleges. For the first fifty years of the century the vast majority of these students were enrolled in black colleges. Black leadership was drawn from the alumni of a relatively small group of southern colleges where "race uplift" issues and sensitivities were explicitly developed. Today more than 70 percent of all black students study in predominantly white colleges. Nearly half of all black students live in their local communities and attend two-year colleges. This educational diaspora has brought new problems and exacerbated persisting ones.[16]

In her study of the black and white college environments, Jacqueline Fleming explored the behavioral and psychological orientation of black female students' views of themselves either as victims of "double jeopardy"—oppressed as both black and female—or as matriarchs—strong, competent, self-reliant, even domineering women. Fleming found there was a significant loss in assertive abilities among black women in black colleges, while those in white colleges believed that they had improved their social skills, including assertiveness, but expressed dissat-

---

[15] Noble (1979).
[16] Mary Frances Berry, "Blacks in Predominantly White Institutions of Higher Learning," in *The State of Black America* (Washington, D.C.: National Urban League, 1983).

isfaction and negative feelings about the total experience. Fleming concluded that each style of response had strong and weak points. Assertiveness "without academic accomplishment and confidence can be a dead end. And even the brightest academic accomplishments can be eroded by social passivity. . . . The most important question . . . is to find the conditions under which the best of both styles can be developed."[17]

Other recent studies reinforce Cuthbert's "marginality syndrome," concluding that black college women bear unique psychological burdens. Many black college women describe feelings of alienation and frustration whenever they attempt to relate to black men and white women with whom they are grouped in affirmative action plans.[18]

Society generally associates higher education degrees with a successful life which includes access to advanced or professional degrees, an esteemed job, a good income, and the choice of a family life. To a lesser extent, service to the community is expected. And considering the historic mission of "race uplift" for blacks, it is reasonable to expect that black women graduates will contribute toward the betterment of the race. How much progress have black college women made in these areas?

A pattern of black women's superiority over black men in degree attainment begins in high school, continues in college, and includes one or two years of graduate work. While black women may outnumber black men in first degrees earned, the prestigious postbaccalaureate degrees that are usually associated with high income, status, and power currently place black men somewhat ahead of black women. This fact has been cited as a "litmus test" to disprove the matriarachy theory and to

[17] Jacqueline Fleming, "Black Women in Black and White College Environments: The Making of a Matriarch," *Journal of Social Issues* 39 (1983): 52.
[18] Joyce Jones and Olga Welch, "The Black Professional Woman: Psychological Consequences of Social and Educational Inequities upon the Achievement of High Status Careers in Leadership Position," *Journal of National Association of Women Deans and Counselors* (Winter 1979): 29–32.

disclaim any superior status black women are believed to have over black men. Yet black women are rapidly closing the educational gap between them and black men on every educational level, and some other explanation to disprove the matriarchy theory must be found.

As opportunities open for women and blacks, black women are diversifying from a heavy concentration in education to nontraditional, better-paying fields. Black men are not diversifying as rapidly as black women. The numbers of black women either exceeded or matched those of black men graduating with baccalaureate degrees in such fields as mathematics, prelaw, computer science, and business management. During this same period black women earned 44 percent of all the professional degrees earned by blacks. In the fields of law and medicine approximately 40 percent of all blacks in the graduating population were women.[19]

The gap between black and white women in educational attainment is greater than that between black men and women. Considerably more white men than white women have attained college degrees, and twice as many attain postbaccalaureate education, obviating any thought of white women's status being superior to white males. The white woman steps into the competitive arena knowing she is striving to reach parity in a white male power situation where males are greatly distanced from her in educational attainment and income. Of course, as long as sexism exists, all women face situations where too many men, white and black, are threatened by ambitious and qualified women. But the threat of women's advancement is particularly anxiety-provoking for so many black men. The close proximity of black men to black women and their overall powerlessness in the larger society constantly remind them that

[19]U.S. Department of Education, Office for Civil Rights, *Data on Earned Degrees Conferred by Institutions of Higher Education by Race, Ethnicity, and Sex, Year 1980–1981* (Washington, D.C.: Government Printing Office, 1982).

more and more they are competing for power and prestige with women—white and black. Far too many feel cheated of opportunities and turn their frustrations toward their own racial sisters.[20]

In thirty years (1950–1980) black college women made consistent progress in entering the labor market with college degrees and diversifying their occupational fields. They entered almost every professional field as opportunities for blacks and women expanded. By 1980 their progress in the fields of medicine, architecture, management, science, and engineering particularly had brought them close to parity with black men. Black women exceed 33 percent of all black scientists. And a stunning 77 percent of blacks and 15 percent of all women are black women employed in the mathematical sciences.[21]

While black women advance, black men continue to experience greater losses in labor force activity than any other group. Yet black men outnumber women three to one as managers and administrators (except farm), creating a visibility in some leadership positions that often beclouds the real facts about declining black male progress in most other occupational positions. Black women lag behind both black men and white women in management positions. Despite a pioneering history of black women in the field of education, little progress has been made in achieving administrative positions in education. Blacks in general are grossly underrepresented in higher education, constituting only 4 percent of college faculties in 1983. Blacks are usually in the lowest ranks, where promotion and tenure are rarely achieved. Yet even among the small number of blacks, black women are the fewest of the few.[22]

Is it racism or sexism that creates the shutout for black

[20] Barbara A. P. Jones, "The Economic Status of Black Women," in *The State of Black America*: 115–154.

[21] Betty M. Vetter and Eleanor L. Babso, *Professional Women and Minorities* (New York: Scientific Manpower Commission, 1984).

[22] Berry, "Blacks in Predominantly White Institutions."

women? It is probably both, forcing black women into a "marginality anxiety," where they acknowledge neither white women nor black men as allies. In this historical period when universities are typically male bastions and a major battleground for white feminists, black women in academe are a small, powerless group. Even in black colleges the plight of black women is dismal. Attitudes of black male colleagues in black institutions are generally and openly accepted by most black women academics as sexist, and some research is beginning to give objective data to support that claim.[23]

In the highest income categories, black men's earnings exceed those of black women and white women. Out of fifteen professional and managerial occupations that usually attract college graduates, black men's median earnings were higher than that of white and black women. In seven of fifteen professional occupations, however, black women's median income exceeded that of white women. Of the remaining eight occupations, the disparity between black and white women's earnings was about $1,000. White women physicians made $4,000 more than black women, but black dentists doubled the median income of white women. In the upper income brackets ($25,000 and over), however, white women appeared to be the only group with a percentage gain in earning higher salaries. Between 1962 and 1982 the percentage gain for black women in higher income brackets remain the same, and men, both black and white, showed a decline.[24]

It would appear that black women have made better progress than black men in educational attainment and entering most professional occupations with the exception of the fields of management and higher education. Black college-educated

[23] Althea Smith and Abigail J. Stewart "Approaches to Studying Racism and Sexism in Black Women's Lives," *Journal of Social Issues* 39 (1983): 1–15; Perkins, "Impact of the Cult of True Womanhood."
[24] U.S. Department of Commerce, *Money Income of Households, Families, and Persons in the U.S.* (Washington, D.C.: Government Printing Office, 1982).

men, though proportionately fewer in number, earn more income than all women. One wonders if the growing sensitivity to the black man's fate might not work to the advantage of those black men who present themselves for promotion in professional fields. Black men may well be overfavored in order to provide male role models or because there is an attitude that black men need more power or money to rectify past injustices. Perhaps it's easier to let a black male into the "ol' boys' club" simply because white men feel more comfortable with other males.

Living a life as a single woman and rearing children without husbands have been dominant themes in the black community for generations. These themes, when translated into current statistics, show a worsening condition. They are fearful possibilities for college women. Since 1940 there has been a downward trend in the proportion of all black families that include both husband and wife (from 77 percent to 61 percent in 1975), declining to 54 percent in 1980. Of all black women 34 percent were never married in 1980.

No black woman goes away to college without knowing how risky her chances are for getting a husband. Should she choose a predominantly white college, she finds herself in a "devastating competition for a very scarce resource." Black women are not really much better off at black colleges, where they outnumber male students, although competition to share scarce resources with white women is seldom a factor.[25]

The influence of loneliness on the psychological development of black college women is of interest to scholars. Does a college education contribute toward the woman's remaining single? Or is the black graduate more attractive as a financial partner because of her earning power?

It seems inevitable that black women will make more visible

[25] Lorenzo Middleton and A. C. Roark, "Lonely Social Life of Black Women on White Campus," *Chronicle of Higher Education* 22 (July 20, 1981).

progress than black men in educational attainment and occupational advancement. "Status superiority" over black men becomes an increasing reality. As young black women move ahead of black men academically, they are often conflicted, confused, and fearful of alienating them. Since interracial dating and marriage are less an option for black women than men, many are concerned that their success may cost them dating and marriage partners. Anxiety and fear that success will lead to loneliness add an emotional burden to young black women as they compete with white women and men for an even greater share of opportunities.

A study conducted in 1976 found that black students (male and female) in black colleges appeared to value "mission goals," such as aiding the community and influencing politics, more than students attending predominantly white institutions. The latter students were more goal-oriented toward affluence and success in business. Current research on "Going for the Oppressed," a theme of "racial upliftment," describes difficulties in studying black middle-class professional women's race consciousness and commitment to use their positions to forward black causes and help black people. The subjects in one study started out working as "uplifters" but discovered that it took a strong will and spirit to maintain that commitment when presented with opportunities for advancement. Co-option by whites is difficult for an occupationally mobile black woman to resist. Strategies of moving ahead while maintaining a black commitment take "extra" time and energy. "Maintaining rootedness in the black community while being upwardly mobile" means for many women limiting the scope of their career satisfactions to the interests of the black community and refusing to dwell on the reward system of the dominant society. Who in this current college black female generation will pay such a price when our society rewards financial and status success?[26]

[26] Berry, "Blacks in Predominantly White Institutions"; Cheril Townsend Gilkes, "Going

In summary, "utilitarian drive" with a strong emphasis on career preparation continues to motivate black women to seek college educations. Since the middle half of the century they have been mainly job-oriented, even at the expense of neglecting an education that aims to develop the whole person and foster self fulfillment. In the eighties the traditional ambition to enter teaching has been replaced by new career interests in a wide variety of professions. As these women have become more and more successful in their occupational mobility, they provide role models for younger black women. It is likely that subsequent generations will also adopt a similar "utilitarian drive" in pursuit of education.

Black college women are advancing ahead of black men in educational attainment and occupational advancement. A "status superiority" does indeed threaten relationships, especially since our society is still controlled by white men. Ignoring the divisive argument of matriarchy, yet suggesting the desirability of working / loving partnerships between black men and women, the college education of black women does increase the likelihood that a black woman will have "status superiority" over black men. This may very well continue to create disharmonious relationships.

Except in the highest income and management levels, black college women are making progress in reaching parity with white women. In their attempts to advance to the upper echelons of business and academia, however, lack of access or discrimination frustrates their progress. Black women feel only "marginally" connected to white women as a group and rarely share a sense of camaraderie with them in the struggle for women's rights.

Black college women have traditionally concerned themselves with the likelihood that college may decrease their mar-

Up for the Oppressed: The Career Mobility of Black Community Workers," *Journal of Social Issues* 39 (1983): 115–39.

riage possibilities. It is very likely that this generation of college women will face an even more difficult time securing mates. In an earlier study Patricia Roberts Harris, who eventually became the first black woman ambassador and cabinet officer, talked about the loneliness black college women experienced in the fifties. Her words are instructive today.

> . . . the experience I have had in the last few years, working with thousands of women, is that many young women are loneliest and feel most unsuited for working with the problems of the community because they have not been able to find the man they have been looking for. They feel until they have that, they cannot move on to the next thing. It seems to me that education, if it is to be effective, must help people to learn how to live wholly their whole life . . . [that] the millions of single women today often lack something which makes it impossible for them to be themselves at their best because they keep thinking they are failures . . . [and] somewhere they have fallen short. They are unable to say, given myself as I am today with whatever friends, relatives, family, community I have, how do I become an effective person. . . .[27]

[27] Quoted in Noble (1956).

ROSALIND ROSENBERG
The Limits of Access:
The History of Coeducation
in America

The roots of collegiate coeducation reach back to the years before the Civil War, when women first gained access to Oberlin and a few other colleges on terms nearly equal to men. This access owed much to the efforts of the early women's rights movement, whose leaders declared that coeducation was an essential precondition of woman's emancipation from her "separate sphere." Disappointed by the education provided at the female secondary schools of their day, early feminists feared that separate education for women would inevitably be inferior to that of men. The only way of ensuring equality, they argued, was to insist that women and men be educated together.[1]

[1] For early women's rights leaders' views on coeducation see Mari Jo Buhle and Paul Buhle, eds., *The Concise History of Woman Suffrage: Selections from the Classic Work of Stanton, Anthony, Gage, and Harper* (Urbana, Ill.: University of Illinois, 1987):

ROSALIND ROSENBERG *is professor of history at Barnard College, New York City.*

Coeducation appealed to the leaders of the early women's movement not simply on academic grounds but on sexual grounds as well. In their view, the segregation of young men and women led to an undue preoccupation with sex; whereas the joint education of the sexes created a more natural and therefore healthier sexual atmosphere. "If the sexes were educated together," argued Elizabeth Cady Stanton, "we should have the healthy, moral and intellectual stimulus of sex ever quickening and refining all the faculties, without the undue excitement of senses that results from novelty in the present system of isolation." Coeducation, then, promised intellectual emancipation and sexual well-being.[2]

Women's early success at Oberlin persuaded many early women's rights leaders that coeducation would soon be achieved throughout the country. Lucy Stone summed up their views in an address at the 1856 Women's Rights Convention in New York City. "Our demand that Harvard and Yale colleges should admit women, though not yet yielded, only waits for a little more time. And while they wait, numerous petty 'female colleges' have sprung into being, indicative of the justice of our claim that a college education should be granted to women. Not one of these female colleges . . . meets the demands of the age, and so will eventually perish."[3]

112, 119, 158, 203; "Coeducation of the Sexes," *Woman's Journal* (September 21, 1872); Charlotte Williams Conable, *Women at Cornell: The Myth of Equal Education* (Ithaca, N.Y.; Cornell University Press, 1977): 26–42. Precedent for collegiate coeducation existed in the academies open to both male and female pupils from the late eighteenth century onward. Though less numerous than the separate institutions, they were well known, and their existence influenced those who pressed for coeducation at the college level. See Thomas Woody, *A History of Women's Education in the United States* (New York: Science Press, 1929): 2:228.

[2] Published in Pauline Wright Davis, *A History of the National Woman's Rights Movement* (New York: 1871): 62, quoted in William Leach, *True Love and Perfect Union: The Feminist Reform of Sex and Society* (New York: Basic Books, 1980): 80.

[3] Quoted in Buhle and Buhle, *Concise History of Woman Suffrage:* 158. On restrictions on women's education at Oberlin, see Ronald Hogeland, "Coeducation of the Sexes at Oberlin College: A Study of Social Ideas in Mid-Nineteenth Century Amer-

Stone could not have been more wrong in her specific pre-
diction. Harvard and Yale did not admit women on equal terms
with men for more than a century, and female colleges, far
from perishing, proliferated and flourished in the years that
followed her speech. Yet in a more general sense Stone was
right. Despite the resistance of Harvard and Yale (and of other
male preserves, especially in the East and South), by the end
of the nineteenth century coeducation had become the predominant form of higher education in this country, and today
more than 95 percent of all college women are enrolled in
coeducational institutions.[4]

What remains uncertain is how fully coeducation lived up
to the hopes of its early advocates. Scholars have written exten-
sively about the history of higher education, but they have
directed little attention to the impact of its predominant form
on women's lives. Only in the past decade have historians begun
to mine the archives of the colleges and universities and to
describe women's experience in a number of different institutions. Much remains to be done, but some patterns have begun
to emerge.

Though advocates of coeducation achieved some success in
the antebellum period, their most important gains came in the
wake of the Civil War, a war that left unprecedented numbers
of young women faced with the necessity of supporting themselves. By 1872 ninety-seven colleges and universities had
decided to admit women. These institutions varied widely in
educational quality and purpose, and most were inferior to the
eastern male colleges. But a significant and growing number

ica," *Journal of Social History* 5 (1972): 160–76. On Oberlin's influence, see Barbara
Solomon, "The Impact of Oberlin's Coeducational Model on Other Colleges," in
Educating Women and Men Together: Coeducation in a Changing World, ed. Carol
Lasser and Sondra J. Peacock (Urbana, Ill.: University of Illinois Press, 1987).
[4] Mabel Newcomer, *A Century of Higher Education for Women* (New York: Harper
and Bros., 1959): 49; Barbara Miller Solomon, *In the Company of Educated Women:
A History of Women and Higher Education in America* (New Haven: Yale University
Press, 1985): 207.

of institutions—including Cornell, the University of Michigan, Wesleyan, Boston University, Wisconsin, and Berkeley—did more than any educational institution ever had to give women the same education offered to men.[5]

Some of these institutions bowed to the power of moral exhortation in deciding to admit women. Boston University, for example, admitted women students in the early 1870s simply because, as President William Warren said, the time had come for the idea of education for men only to be "retired to the museum of pedagogical paleontology." At Cornell coeducation grew out of a long campaign, conducted by both male and female women's rights advocates, including Horace Greeley, Elizabeth Cady Stanton, Susan B. Anthony, and Maria Mitchell.[6] Typically, however, the reasons for implementing coeducation were more complex. One compelling reason was the growing need for women teachers. Plagued by labor scarcity and indebtedness, many communities found it difficult to recruit teachers. In their search for cheap labor they hired women and urged legislatures to provide them with adequate training. A second encouraging factor was the 1862 passage of the Morrill Land Grant Act, by which Congress fostered the growth of the state universities. As these institutions developed, taxpayers demanded that their daughters, as well as their sons, be admitted. The University of Wisconsin began training women as teachers in its normal school during the Civil War, when male enrollment plummeted, and the University of Michigan adopted coeducation in 1870, when the legislature forced a reluctant administration to accept women rather than undertake the extra expense of building a separate school.[7]

---

[5]Woody, A *History of Women's Education:* 2:251–2; Patricia Albjerg Graham, "Expansion and Exclusion: A History of Women in Higher Education," *Signs* 3 (1978): 761; Leach, *True Love and Perfect Union:* 71–72.
[6]Warren O. Ault, *Boston University: The College of Liberal Arts, 1873–1973* (Boston: Boston University, 1973): 7; Conable, *Women at Cornell:* 26–61.
[7]Woody, A *History of Women's Education:* 2: 230–47; Helen M. Olin, *Women of a*

These factors helped determine the pattern of coeducation's successes and failures. In the East, where men's schools like Harvard and Yale were firmly established and where benefactors provided funds for separate instruction for women, coeducation made inroads. In the Midwest and West, where financial pressures tended to be greater, coeducation became the norm. The South represented a partial exception that confirmed this general economic rule. As a consequence of the Civil War and the conservative social tradition that lingered in the South, collegiate education developed more slowly than in the rest of the country, and sexual segregation persisted longer in both public and private institutions. Where traditions were weaker and economic constraints pronounced, however, coeducation was adopted. Thus, coeducation in the South came first to the state universities of Texas, Arkansas, and Mississippi and to the black colleges. Only slowly did it spread eastward to the old South, not reaching the state-supported University of Virginia until 1970.[8]

To the early leaders of the women's movement coeducation was a matter of right, but to those who finally relented coeducation was more often a matter of expediency, adopted simply because the separate education of women was too costly. This economic reality soured the coeducational experience from the start, for many male students regarded the presence of women students as a constant reminder of their second-class status with respect to eastern male schools. Women students were further hampered in their efforts to win acceptance by

State University (New York: Putnam, 1909): 22–47; Dorothy Dies McGuigan, *A Dangerous Experiment: 100 Years of Women at the University of Michigan* (Ann Arbor, Mich.: University of Michigan, 1970): 15–30.

[8] Rosalind Rosenberg, *Beyond Separate Spheres: Intellectual Roots of Modern Feminism* (New Haven: Yale University Press, 1982): 30–31; Elizabeth Lee Ihle, "The Development of Coeducation in Major Southern State Universities" (Ph.D. thesis, University of Tennessee, Knoxville, 1976): 101–178; Patricia A. Stringer and Irene Thompson, eds., *Stepping Off the Pedestal: Academic Women in the South* (New York: Modern Language Association, 1982): 148–49.

having to enter a male domain already well established. Male college culture in the late nineteenth century was marked by a good deal of rowdyism and brawling, much of which centered on the tradition of the "freshman-sophomore feud." At Michigan, Berkeley, and other schools across the country fights between freshmen and sophomore men could erupt at any time in chapel, in corridors, even in classrooms, and the faculty seemed helpless to stop the antagonists. Supporters of coeducation often argued that the presence of women would have a civilizing effect on male students, but that contention ignored the reality of strongly entrenched male traditions combined with the fact that men made up a large majority of the student bodies at coeducational schools.[9]epInstitutions that were coeducational from their founding, as were Boston University (1869) and the University of Chicago (1892), generally succeeded more readily in integrating women and men than did institutions that simply added women to an already established male student body. At Wesleyan, where many male students complained that coeducation had been foisted on them by misguided administrators, men devised a variety of tactics to display their displeasure. They beat any men seen talking to a female student, barred women from appearing in the yearbook, and excluded them from membership in student organizations. Whether women's presence was generally accepted or not, however, they remained a group apart. As pictures of lecture halls reveal, a fairly strict pattern of segregation prevailed, with women seated on one side of the room, men seated on the other.[10]

[9]McGuigan, A *Dangerous Experiment:* 44; Lynn D. Gordon, "Co-education on Two Campuses: Berkeley and Chicago, 1890–1912," in *Woman's Being, Woman's Place: Female Identity and Vocation in American History*, ed. Mary Kidley (Boston: G. K. Hall, 1979): 173; "Stanford's First Women Students," *Stanford Observer* (May 1985): 3.
[10]Louise Wilby Knight, "The 'Quails': The History of Wesleyan University's First Period of Coeducation, 1872–1912" (Honors thesis, Wesleyan University, 1972): 30–

Women generally tolerated the uncivil behavior of their male classmates with dignified disdain; in fact, they were sometimes amused "to hear a boy of nineteen or twenty years define woman's sphere, and mark the line which she shall or ought to walk." The prejudice of male professors, however, proved more unsettling. Many professors had resisted the admission of women, citing studies which purported to show that women were physically incapable of higher education, and some professors found it difficult to acknowledge women's presence once they were admitted. At Boston University some professors treated women students as trespassers, addressing them by their last names. At Michigan one instructor addressed his "mixed class of men and women as 'gentlemen,' and, in calling on a woman student addressed her as 'Mr. so-and-so,' as though he were still teaching an all male class." Ignoring women's presence sometimes took the extreme form of denying them the conventional honors of academic achievement. As industrial engineer Lillian Moller Gilbreth recalled of her experience at Berkeley in 1900, "There was no prejudice against women students. Consequently, it was a surprise, and a painful one, to aim for a Phi Beta Kappa key, only to learn there would be no girls on the list because 'when it came to finding a job, men needed the help of this honor more than women did.' " Having access to the same education as men did not always entail being accorded the same right of recognition. [11]

Women's minority status on many campuses was underscored by the facilities available for their use. The spacious dormitories and well-equipped gymnasiums of the eastern women's colleges rarely existed for women at coeducational institutions before 1900. On most campuses men had filled

47, 117–22; Margaret Rossiter, *Women Scientists in America: Struggles and Strategies to 1940* (Baltimore: Johns Hopkins, 1982): 10.

[11] Ault, *Boston University*: 8; McGuigan, A *Dangerous Experiment*: 32; "Lillian Moller Gilbreth," in *There Was Light: Autobiography of a University, Berkeley: 1868–1969,* ed. Irving Stone (New York: Doubleday, 1970): 83.

the little dormitory space available when female students entered, so women had to join the overflow of male students in boardinghouses off campus. Those schools that could afford to build gymnasium or a student center typically either barred women from both or strictly limited their access.[12]

In retrospect, the faith of early women's rights leaders that the admittance of women to men's colleges would lead to the abolition of woman's "separate sphere" within American higher education seems naive. Early feminists simply underestimated the tenacity of the male collegiate tradition in the face of a feminine incursion that few men welcomed. Yet despite the difficulties women endured, coeducation gave them the satisfaction of knowing that they could meet the same educational challenges faced by their brothers. As President James B. Angell observed of the Michigan woman student, "there is a value in the consciousness she has that her education is identical in scope and thoroughness with that of her brother; that circumstance gives her confidence, self-reliance and strength." Conditioned from childhood to doubt her own intelligence, the woman admitted to a male institution had the pleasure of discovering that she could match or surpass the achievements of male students.[13]

Along with their sense of intellectual accomplishment, the pioneers of coeducation enjoyed an unusual degree of personal freedom. Many universities permitted women to come and go as they pleased, just as men did, and despite the "anti-coed" policy often adopted by student organizations, friendships between men and women proved difficult to prevent. As the heroine of an early roman à clef about life at Michigan commented in a letter to a Vassar friend:

> Now you wanted to know about the boys—whether they pay us much attention . . . Well, I'll just tell you that you could not

[12] Gordon, "Co-education on Two Campuses": 173–75; McGuigan, A *Dangerous Experiment*: 43, 59; Ihle, "Development of Coeducation": 103, 107, 126.
[13] McGuigan, A *Dangerous Experiment*: 42.

carry on many flirtations, and keep up your standing in class too. Some of the girls tried it, but found they must give up one or the other, and with remarkable good sense they chose their books instead of the boys. Yet from the way the wind blows, I should not wonder if one or two matches were made in our class. Well, what could be more natural and fitting? Where can men and women learn to know each other better than by reciting in the same classes? Why did not your father let you come here with me, instead of sending you off to an old boarding-school, where you don't see a fellow once a month, and are always watched by some old corridor spy?

The first generation of college women was a dedicated group, more interested in preparing for a career than in finding a husband, more inclined to seek fellowship with each other than with men. But roughly half the women married, and those trained at coeducational institutions often married men from the same institution. Even at Wesleyan, where the ostracism of female students from student life was particularly severe, one-third of the women married Wesleyan men.[14]

In the 1870s and 1880s women represented a small minority of the students at coeducational institutions. But by 1900 the popularity of higher education among women had become so great that female enrollment at many colleges and universities outstripped male enrollment. There swept through the country a growing fear that if nothing were done to prevent it, within a few years many coeducational institutions would become women's schools. Schools that had welcomed women when they represented an economic asset now worried that American universities had been saved from the fate of insolvency only to be subjected to the much worse fate of "femini-

---

[14] Olive San Louie Anderson, *An American Girl and Her Four Years in a Boys' College* (1878), quoted in McGuigan, A *Dangerous Experiment*: 50–51; Mary Roberts Coolidge, "Statistics of College and Non-College Women," *American Statistical Association* 7 (March–June 1900): 19–20; Knight, "The 'Quails' ": 38. Two-thirds of the women at Wesleyan married.

zation." This fear led many colleges and universities to reconsider their coeducational policy.[15]

At the University of Chicago some faculty and administrators argued that they had never really favored coeducation in the first place but had agreed to it merely for economic reasons. Now that Chicago was firmly established as a prestigious university, continuing to admit women simply served, as one professor remarked, "to divert . . . a large number of the best class of college men" to all-male schools like Yale. A minority of the faculty fought the administration's proposal to segregate men and women in their freshman and sophomore years, but to no avail. At Stanford University the founder's widow so feared that the university, dedicated to the memory of her son, would become a female seminary that she froze female enrollment permanently at 500. Boston University launched a "More Men Movement" to try to persuade young men to enroll in greater numbers. And Wesleyan simply abandoned coeducation altogether.[16]

The turn-of-the-century reaction against coeducation drew energy from the widespread perception that the women students coming to college were distinctly less serious than earlier women students had been. Whereas the first generation of women who attended such institutions as Michigan and Cornell were strongly committed to careers, at the expense, if necessary, of family life, the next generation represented a broader group of young women, many of whom regarded college not simply as an avenue to work but also as preparation for marriage. Marion Talbot, dean of women at Chicago, described the less ambitious young women coming to college after 1900 in a speech to a group of club women: "An increasing number are entering college who have no interest in research or even

[15] Woody, *A History of Women's Education*: 2: 280–95.
[16] Rosenberg, *Beyond Separate Spheres*: 45; C. W. Elliot, *Stanford University: The First Twenty-Five Years* (Stanford: Stanford University Press, 1937): 132–36; Ault, *Boston University*: 94; Knight, "The 'Quails' ": 142–55.

in careful but not advanced scholarship." Talbot conceded that these new, less ambitious students "still have the desire within them to make the most of themselves," but she warned her listeners that colleges were inevitably limited in what they could accomplish by the values and aspirations instilled in students by society and their families. A college could not make a scholar out of a student who had no ambition to be one.[17]

The rapid rise in female enrollment, together with the more diverse character of the female student body, persuaded many university officials that they could no longer dismiss women students as exceptions or rely on mutual hostility between the sexes to preserve Victorian morality. Schools that had consciously refrained from passing any special regulations for women in the early years of coeducation began hiring deans to supervise their women students. At Michigan President Angell, having declined to hire a dean for more than two decades, finally submitted to pressure from the regents in 1896 to hire someone to exercise "intellectual and moral oversight" over the women students. Angell chose Eliza Mosher, one of Michigan's most outstanding early women medical school graduates, and offered her a post as full professor of hygiene in the Literary college. Mosher took her responsibility for "moral oversight" seriously, devising elaborate rules for social conduct and enforcing them zealously. Young women traveling to and from college, for instance, were required to travel by day if they were going by coach and by Pullman sleeper if at night. Once a freshman going home for vacation sat up all night in a coach, and Mosher promptly suspended her from school.[18]

One of the biggest problems suffered by coeducational institutions, suddenly convinced of the need to enforce sexual segregation in student life, was that they did not have enough dormitory space to house all their students. Suddenly women

---

[17] Marion Talbot, "Cooperation in Educational Methods Between College and Club Women," *Journal of the Association of Collegiate Alumnae* 3 (February 1906): 36.
[18] McGuigan, *A Dangerous Experiment:* 59–68.

whose housing and athletic needs had been ignored for decades found themselves the beneficiaries of new dormitories and gymnasiums. Students gave these new structures a mixed response. Many women rejoiced at finally being able to enjoy the kind of fellowship and physical activity that the men had enjoyed all along. Others regretted the loss of freedom, the indignity of submitting to rules fashioned only for women, and the new distance established between the sexes. At Grinnell College, male students protested the cloistering of women students in a new set of dormitories. "The natural social relations between men and women, always somewhat warped in the college atmosphere, has been almost completely thwarted by artificial barriers," complained one man. No longer able to eat together, men and women found it difficult, under the new system of segregated housing, to form a wide circle of friendships.[19]

Women's heightened presence in coeducational institutions led not only to changes in campus social life but also to a reconsideration of the education women should receive. The idea that women should be trained differently from men was an old one, but until the turn of the century women faculty and women's rights leaders had opposed it. As higher education came to appeal to a broader spectrum of young womanhood, however, courses fitted to women's domestic interests gained support, not only from male educators but from female educators as well.

The experience of Marion Talbot provides an interesting case study of the complicated forces that lay behind the emergence of "women's courses" in coeducational institutions. Talbot, one of Boston University's first women graduates in 1880, took her master's degree in chemistry with Ellen Rich-

[19] Joan G. Zimmerman, "Daughters of Main Street: Culture and the Female Community at Grinnell 1884–1917," in *"Women's Being, Women's Place*: 167; Gordon, "Co-education on Two Campuses": 174–75; Ihle, "Development of Coeducation": 103, 107, 126, 127–28.

ards at the Massachusetts Institute of Technology in 1884. Briefly she taught at Wellesley and then moved in 1892 to Chicago to serve as dean of women and assistant professor of sociology. There she tried to persuade President William Rainey Harper to allow her to establish a department of sanitary science to train both men and women to deal with the problems of urban planning, sanitation, and consumer protection. She envisioned a program that would include courses in chemistry, physics, physiology, political economy, and modern languages—a program that would enable women and men to work together to alleviate urban problems. Because he had overcommitted his funds, Harper denied Talbot's request, urging her to work for her goals within the department of sociology. [20]

In the beginning sociology proved a sympathetic home for Talbot and her plans. Though the men in the department thought of themselves as scholars more than as reformers, they assumed that there was an intimate connection between scientific study and reform activity. But as the university expanded, professional ambition, combined with the belief that specialization was necessary to scientific advance, led them away from interdisciplinary and reformist activity. [21]

By 1902 Talbot had had to abandon her initial hope that sanitary science could become the central focus of the social and physical sciences in the reform of urban society. A steady stream of letters from expanding state universities asking for recommendations for teachers of home economics, the shifting character of women students at Chicago, and her colleagues' growing concern with specialization, combined to persuade Talbot that she should narrow her claim to academic expertise from sanitary science to home economics. Two years later Harper eliminated the field of sanitary science within sociology and established a separate department, called house-

[20] Rosenberg, *Beyond Separate Spheres*: 35.
[21] Ibid: 35, 49.

hold administration, under Talbot's direction. Although Talbot gained the independence she had been seeking for more than a decade, the very title of the department Harper finally bestowed upon her eliminated the androgynous tone of the field she had first sought to create. Thus, the dramatic rise in women students' enrollment merged with the trend toward specialization to reinforce traditional attitudes about women's role in American society and to cut short the curricular reforms that some of the more farsighted female academics sought to foster.[22]

In many ways, then, the years between 1900 and 1910 represented a retreat from the early feminist vision of a life free of sex segregation. As student bodies became more broadly representative of the American populace and as men within academia struggled to secure a position of strength amid the female invasion, it became harder to distinguish the coeducational experience from life in the larger society. As new disciplines developed, men and women became concentrated in different fields within them. Experimental psychology became men's work; clinical psychology and social work became women's work.[23]

Many scholars, pointing to the disproportionately large number of successful women scientists produced by the elite women's colleges, have argued that the separate education deplored by early feminists actually did more to challenge conventional gender roles than did mixed education. But other scholars have suggested that graduates of the Seven Sisters owed their interest in science more to their relatively privileged backgrounds than to separate education by itself. A comparison of course enrollment figures in 1900 at such roughly comparable institutions as Chicago and Wellesley suggests that, for these two schools at least, the willingness of women students

[22] Ibid: 49.
[23] Alice I. Bryan and Edwin G. Boring, "Women in American Psychology: Factors Affecting Their Professional Careers," *American Psychologist* 2 (January 1947): 3–21.

to challenge prevailing stereotypes was about the same whether they studied with men or not. In both schools roughly 35 percent of the women studied foreign languages, while only about 15 percent studied the physical sciences and mathematics. More recent comparisons of single sex and coeducational institutions suggest that women at coeducational institutions are slightly *more* likely to take courses in traditionally masculine fields than their sisters at women's colleges. Moreover, studies that have taken the social and economic background of students into account suggest that graduates of women's colleges have not been any more likely to pursue careers after college than graduates of coeducational institutions. The expectations that young women bring to college and the opportunities available to them at college and in the larger world may be more important in their choice of courses than the presence or absence of men. [24]

Whatever the ultimate verdict on which type of institution succumbed more completely to the social pressure to prepare women students for conventional roles, scholars generally agree that neither form ever encouraged so extreme a pattern of sex segregation as the society from which it grew. American colleges and universities opened doors never before opened to women, and many students walked through to lives women never had experienced before. Despite the continuing tendency of women and men to concentrate in different kinds of work, higher education greatly broadened women's opportu-

[24] Rossiter, *Women Scientists in America:* 1–28; M. Elizabeth Tidball, "Baccalaureate Origins of American Scientists and Scholars," *Science* 193 (1976): 646–52; Marion Talbot, "The Women of the University," *The Presidents' Report* (Chicago: 1900): 143. See also the debate on college curricula in the *Journal of the Association of Collegiate Alumnae* 3 (December 1898): 1–39. Brown University, *Men and Women Learning Together: A Study of College Students in the Late 1970s,* Report of the Brown Project (April 1980): 112; Mary J. Oates and Susan Williamson, "Women's Colleges and Women Achievers," *Signs* 3 (1978): 795–806; M. Elizabeth Tidball, "Women's Colleges and Woman Achievers Revisited," *Signs* 5 (1980): 504–17; Janet Z. Giele, "Coeducation or Women's Education: New Findings of a Perennial Question," in *Educating Men and Women Together.*

nities. In the mid-1880s, when women students were most enthusiastic about academic experimentation, the great majority became teachers; in the 1910s, even though some of the early iconoclasm had dissipated, women were preparing for a much wider range of occupations. A college education meant that a woman was more likely to work, even if married, and more likely to work in a field traditionally dominated by men. In a society highly segregated by sex, higher education, no matter what its form, provided one of the most important challenges to that segregation.[25]

That challenge grew stronger as the male traditions, which had initially isolated women in many colleges and universities, began to fade and the modern sexual revolution struck American campuses. Ironically, changes in the mores of a new generation of college students rendered largely futile the frantic efforts of university administrators to impose a system of separate sexual spheres on student social life. Reared in a more affluent time than their parents, the youth of the teens and twenties rejected the rigid constraints of Victorian society. Young women cut their hair, threw away their corsets, shortened their skirts, danced all night, and even Eliza Mosher could not do much about it.

The revolt of the younger generation against the proscriptions of their parents permanently altered campus life, especially on coeducational campuses. One young woman at Ohio State University summed up the new sense of freedom in her school newspaper:

> The college girl—particularly the girl in the coeducational institution—is a plucky, coolheaded individual who thinks naturally.

[25] Mary Van Kleeck, "A Census of College Women," *Journal of the Association of Collegiate Alumnae* 11 (May 1918): 561; Julie Matthaei, *An Economic History of Women in America: Women's Work, the Sexual Division of Labor, and the Development of Capitalism* (New York: Schocken, 1982): 285–93; Solomon, *In the Company of the Educated Women:* 115–40.

She doesn't lose her head—she knows her game and can play it dextrously. She is armed with sexual knowledge. . . . She is secure in the most critical situations—she knows the limits, and because of her safety in such knowledge she is able to run almost the complete gamut of experience.

Elizabeth Cady Stanton had not intended that coeducation be as "natural" as the Ohio student found it to be, but surely she would have applauded the young woman's belief in her power to control her own body.[26]

The impact of the sexual revolution varied greatly in different groups. Small Catholic and black colleges continued to demand adherence to strict rules of conduct, both on and off campus, but most large schools abandoned the effort to chaperon students at all times. A small measure of the extent of the change in student life may be seen in the fact that even at Cornell, where men had observed an unwritten law against dating their female classmates for decades, fraternities began to admit coeds to their parties in the 1920s. As one Cornell woman later recalled, "The thing I remember about social life was the big difference between the coeds and the imports at parties, when they came for weekends. They had such a different attitude towards men. We were much more matter-of-fact. My sister at Wellesley didn't have a date for an evening the way we did. She always had a date for a weekend and very often, she'd say that she never wanted to see that guy again." Many observers deplored the seeming decline in academic seriousness among the young and regretted the tendency of younger college women to be valued more for their social desirability than their intelligence. But college women had gained something important in the relaxation of sexual mores

[26] *Ohio State Lantern* (January 9, 1922), quoted in Paula Fass, *The Damned and the Beautiful: American Youth in the 1920s* (New York: Oxford University Press, 1977): 307.

in the early twentieth century. No longer did attending college mark one as a social pariah.[27]

The teens and twenties were years of promise for college women, and that promise seemed especially strong within coeducational institutions because of their rapid expansion. English Professor Marjorie Nicolson, a graduate of the University of Michigan, who went on to hold professorships at Vassar and then Columbia, recalled the years during and after World War I as the best ever for women in higher education:

> We came late enough to escape the self-consciousness and the belligerence of the pioneers, to take education and training for granted. We came early enough to take equally for granted professional positions in which we could make full use of our training. This was our double glory; it never occurred to us at the time that we were taken only because men were not available . . . [and] woman after woman went into occupations in which they found little limitation imposed because of sex.[28]

In the late nineteenth and early twentieth centuries the women's colleges stood virtually alone in offering faculty positions to talented women; women seeking academic careers found little opportunity in coeducational institutions. But after 1910 the trend shifted. Women's colleges no longer absorbed the number of women they had at their founding. Moreover, in an effort to provide their students with a more "balanced" education, they began replacing retiring women faculty with men. The principal opportunities for women shifted to the land-grant colleges, which expanded rapidly in the teens and twenties. No longer able to attract male faculty as easily as before,

[27] Conable, *Women at Cornell:* 164; Lois K. M. Rosenberry, "Have Women Students Affected the Standards of Coeducational Institutions?," *Journal of the American Association of University Professors* 20 (1927): 37–40.
[28] Marjorie Nicholson, "The Rights and Privileges Pertaining Thereto," *Journal of the American Association of University Women* 31 (1938): 136.

because of a decline in professorial salaries and a concomitant expansion of opportunities in business, land-grant colleges hired women in significant numbers for the first time.[29] By 1930 women represented 28 percent of American college faculties. Despite these remarkable gains, women were rarely hired at the most prestigious institutions. Moreover, they tended to cluster in the lower ranks and in predominantly female departments. The field of home economics alone, for instance, claimed 60 percent of all women faculty members. The reasons for women's failure to make further gains than they did are complex. First, many men were reluctant to hire and promote women, for they feared, as had the male students of the 1870s, that being associated with women raised doubts about one's professional status. Physicist Robert Millikan expressed this fear in a letter written to block the hiring of a woman in the physics department at Duke University in 1936: "I would expect the more brilliant and able young men to be drawn into the graduate department by the character of the men on the staff, rather than the character of the women." One might justify admitting women as students, for they brought in money. But hiring women as faculty and advancing them to higher positions undermined an institution's effort to attract the best young men.[30]

Second, women in academia who sought to advance had to fulfill increasingly more stringent professional expectations, expectations fashioned mostly by men, who had wives ready to assume all the other responsibilities of their lives. When the early women's rights advocates imagined women's working equally with men in medicine, law, and academe, they were thinking of a very different kind of professionalism from the kind that developed in the twentieth century. As education

[29] Susan B. Carter, "Academic Women Revisited: An Empirical Study of Changing Patterns in Women's Employment As College and University Faculty," *Journal of Social History* 14 (1981): 675–99; Rossiter, *Women Scientists* in America: 175–80.
[30] Rossiter, *Women Scientists in America*: 192–93.

became lengthier and more costly, and as professions came to require greater commitment, women suffered. Writing a solid thesis no longer sufficed; one must pursue a research agenda in addition to fulfilling one's teaching duties. [31]

Third, the increasing tendency of women to marry and combine family lives with careers complicated their lives, even as it enriched them. Women who married and had children were caught between the demands of their families and their own teaching and research interests. If an academic woman married an academic man, she faced the added obstacle of nepotism rules that barred her from working in the same institution as her husband. As one embittered woman reported to the Association of Collegiate Alumnae:

> [in graduate school] we were thrown together in our work as well as in our play. We were in every sense equals. . . . From graduate school we went to a state university located in a town of 15,000 inhabitants. My husband had an assistant professorship with a salary of $1,800. We were both enthusiastic about our new prospects. . . . I had come to this place with better equipment, as far as training goes, than any one in my field who was teaching there. But we had been in the town only a short time when we learned of a ruling which eliminated wives of members of the faculty from teaching in the university. [32]

Some historians have argued that after 1920 college-educated women traded the desire to have a career for the desire to have a family life, but this does not square with the available evidence. College-educated women married in greater numbers, but their commitment to careers did not diminish, even after the decline in feminist enthusiasm had robbed them of

[31] Graham, "Expansion and Exclusion": 767–73; Nicolson, "Rights and Privileges Pertaining Thereto": 138–42.
[32] "Reflections of a Professor's Wife," *Journal of the Association of Collegiate Alumnae* 14 (1921): 90.

valuable political support. Each generation of college graduates proved more ready than the last to pursue a career after
marriage, despite widespread public opposition to the practice,
especially during the Great Depression. In the 1920s somewhere between 10 and 28 percent did so; by the 1960s the
proportion had grown to more than half of all women graduates. Whether women attended college with or without men
made little difference in this regard.[33]

Women's employment in academia reflected this overall
trend, with one notable exception: Women's share of employment grew until 1940 but declined after 1947. Returning male
veterans, supported by the GI Bill and attracted by the sharply
higher salaries of the postwar years, made ever greater claims
on the academic market place, while women, weary of depression and war, experienced a temporary but notable drop in
professional aspirations. The impact of veteran preference limited further progress for women in academia for the next two
decades.

Within the past twenty years, however, female scholars, with
the encouragement of a revived women's movement, have more
than redressed those losses. The rapid expansion of higher
education in the 1960s and the capitulation of such remaining
bastions of male exclusivity as Harvard, Princeton, and Yale
to the growing popularity of coeducation provided women with
unprecedented opportunities. In 1963 only 11 percent of all
Ph.D.'s went to women, but by 1983, 33 percent were earned
by women. Moreover, by 1983 women held 36 percent of all
assistant professorships.[34]

Yet despite women's success within coeducation, they remain
subordinate figures within it. That subordination stems from
the legacy of women's restricted access to coeducation as well

[33] Solomon, *In the Company:* 177; Giele, "Coeducation or Women's Education."
[34] Carter, "Academic Women Revisited": 681–83; Jessie Bernard, *Academic Women*
(New York: Meridian, 1964): 29–40; Andrew Hacker, "The Decline of Higher Education," *New York Review of Books* (February 13, 1986): 40.

as from the limited nature of what access can accomplish by itself. Throughout most of the past century women's collegiate enrollment was restricted, officially, as at Stanford, or by social pressure. Only in the 1980s has women's attendance at college come to equal that of men.

At the faculty level, however, women remain a minority. Thus, the world the woman student enters continues to be a world shaped predominantly by men. These men have often proved to be highly successful at challenging their women students intellectually, yet as recent studies at Barnard College and Brown University have shown, female students tend to find role models more frequently from among the female faculty. As a consequence, female students may be less likely to find inspiration in coeducational settings than in the few remaining women's colleges where women faculty are more common.[35]

In sum the rising number of women at all levels of the academy creates a necessary but by no means sufficient condition for realizing the egalitarian vision of coeducation's early advocates. Only changes within liberal education itself can do that. A century ago women were grafted onto an institution built for men in a society dominated by men. Coeducation gave women the opportunity to be more like their brothers. This was a laudable goal in a society that had long reserved its richest prizes for males, but it was a limiting goal as well, for it ignored the concerns, the insights, and the aspirations born of women's differing experiences. During the past decade the study of women in history, anthropology, philosophy, and literary criticism has revealed the male-centered focus of traditional knowledge. In the process "feminization," which at the turn of the century referred to the debasement of a once-proud learned society, has today taken on a new meaning. Thought-

[35] Brown University, *Men and Women Learning Together*: 247; Mirra Komarovsky, *Women in College: Shaping Feminine Identities* (New York: Basic Books, 1985): 306–307.

ful scholars are showing how the study of women and gender not only enriches our knowledge but also transforms how we think about knowledge itself and the society that nurtures it. The ability of coeducation to live up to the expectations of its early advocates turns ultimately, therefore, not on women's reaching statistical parity within academe but on the willingness of the academy to foster this rethinking and to meet its challenge to transform liberal learning.[36]

[36] Florence Howe, *Myths of Coeducation: Selected Essays, 1964–1983* (Bloomington, Ind.: University of Indiana, 1984): 206–220; Carol Berkin, "Clio in Search of Her Daughters/Women in Search of Their Past," *Liberal Education* (Association of American Colleges) 71 (1985): 214.

BARBARA SICHERMAN

College and Careers:

Historical Perspectives on the

Lives and Work Patterns of

Women College Graduates

Despite a burgeoning literature on women's higher education, the relationship between college attendance and employment has received little thoughtful attention by historians.[1] This

[1] A notable exception is Barbara Miller Solomon, *In the Company of Educated Women: A History of Women and Higher Education in America* (New Haven: Yale University Press, 1985): esp. 115–40, 172–85. See also Geraldine Joncich Clifford, " 'Shaking Dangerous Questions from the Crease': Gender and American Higher Education," *Feminist Issues* (Fall 1983): 3–62, and Mabel Newcomer, *A Century of Higher Education for American Women* (New York: Harper, 1959). On vocational training in secondary schools, see Geraldine Joncich Clifford, " 'Marry, Stitch, Die, or Do Worse': Educating Women for Work," in *Work, Youth, and Schooling: Historical Perspectives on Vocationalism in American Education*, ed. Harvey Kantor and David B. Tyack (Stanford: Stanford University Press, 1982): 223–268, and John L. Rury, "Vocationalism for Home and Work: Women's Education in the United States," *History of Education Quarterly* 24 (Spring 1984): 21–44. For a useful recent review of women's education, see Sally Schwager, "Educating Women in America," *Signs* 12 (Winter

BARBARA SICHERMAN *is William R. Kenan, Jr., Professor of American Institutions and Values at Trinity College, Hartford, Connecticut.*

neglect has been fostered in part by the scholarly separation of
the history of higher education from the history of the professions, indeed, from labor history generally. Students of higher
education have by and large concentrated on the undergraduate years (even here the stated goals of founders and presidents
have taken precedence over actual behavior, and extracurricular activities over the curriculum,[2] while studies of the
professions have often highlighted those fields in which women
were a minority, such as medicine, science, and academe,
and have concentrated principally on professional leaders. The
"ordinary" college graduate has thus been lost in the shuffle.

Historians of women in the workplace have charted a cycli-
cal pattern of achievement, emphasizing the late nineteenth
century as a period of unusual attainment by professional (mainly
college) women, followed by a "falling off" (and later by a
resurgence in the wake of the recent women's movement).[3]

1987): 333–72. I wish to thank the following individuals for sharing ideas and mate-
rials: Joyce Antler, Janet Zollinger Giele, Patricia Albjerg Graham, Gail Kilman,
James McLachlan, Norman Miller, Mary Oates, Patricia Palmieri, Linda Perkins,
Tiziana Rota, Michael P. Sacks, Sally Schwager, Barbara Miller Solomon, Susan
Ware, and Francille Wilson. I am especially grateful for helpful comments on the
text by Ruth Bordin, Joan Hedrick, Florence Howe, Janet W. James, Elizabeth Pleck,
Dorothy Ross, Joan W. Scott, Martha Vicinus, and, most of all, Joan Jacobs Brum-
berg, Faye Dudden, and Linda Kerber. Lexa Edsall, Ellen Holtzman, and Debra
Sterling assisted with research.
[2] See, for example, Roberta Frankfort, *Collegiate Women: Domesticity and Career in
Turn-of-the-Century America* (New York: New York University Press, 1977); Joyce
Antler, "Culture, Service, and Work: Changing Ideals of Higher Education for
Women," *The Undergraduate Woman: Issues in Educational Equity*, ed. Pamela J.
Perun (Lexington, Mass.: Lexington Books, 1982): 15–41; and Helen Lefkowitz
Horowitz, *Alma Mater: Design and Experience in the Women's Colleges from Their
Nineteenth-Century Beginnings to the 1930s* (New York: Knopf, 1984).
[3] Jessie Bernard, *Academic Women* (State College, Pa.: Pennsylvania State University
Press, 1964); Patricia M. Hummer, *The Decade of Elusive Promise: Professional Women
in the United States, 1920–1930* (N.p.: UMI Research Press, 1978); Lois Scharf, *To
Work and to Wed: Female Employment, Feminism, and the Great Depression* (West-
port, Conn.: Greenwood Press, 1980); William Henry Chafe, *The American Woman:
Her Changing Social, Economic, and Political Roles, 1920–1970* (New York: Oxford
University Press, 1972): 89–111.

The falling off has been measured by the declining proportion of women taking baccalaureate degrees or working in prestigious professions and has been variously dated to the 1920s, 1930s, or post-war War II era. The purported decline in educational and professional attainment has been broadly linked to cultural and demographic factors, in particular to women's desire for sexual and personal liberation during the 1920s and to the greater emphasis on marriage and childbearing in the 1940s and 1950s. Recent critics of this approach have observed that the absolute number of women in various professions continued to rise even as proportions fell and have suggested that economic and structural factors have as much influence as motivation in determining women's share of employment in a given field.[4]

Ironically, the historical debate on women's professional "progress" has reproduced the central dualism of nineteenth-century discourse on women's work: the incompatibility between paid employment and marriage. Opponents of higher education for women originally insisted that college would "unsex" women—that is, unfit them for their "true" careers as wives and mothers. While rejecting the negative valuation of singlehood, most professional women at the end of the century adhered to a similarly dualistic approach and viewed marriage and career as mutually exclusive alternatives. Scholars have postulated a direct relationship between rising marriage and birth rates among college graduates and diminished labor force participation.[5] This approach not only fails to explain such historical trends as the fall in birth rates and women's partici-

---

[4] Frank Stricker, "Cookbooks and Law Books: The Hidden History of Career Women in Twentieth Century America," *Journal of Social History* 10 (Fall 1976): 1–19, and Susan B. Carter, "Academic Women Revisited: An Empirical Study of Changing Patterns in Women's Employment as College and University Faculty, 1890–1963," *Journal of Social History* 14 (Summer 1981): 675–99.

[5] See Frankfort, *Collegiate Women*, and Bernard, *Academic Women*. For a critique, see Stricker, "Cookbooks and Lawbooks": 7–9.

pation in some professions during the 1930s or the rise in both birth and employment rates in the 1950s but also ignores the impact of changing life course patterns on women's employment.[6] Women's lives have always been more complex than the reigning ideology has decreed.

This article attempts to provide a framework for a more complex understanding of the long-range employment trends of college-educated women. It will do so by drawing on alumnae surveys—a source that has been insufficiently utilized by historians—and by critically examining recent scholarship on women's higher education, much of it scattered in articles and dissertations. Using a life course perspective, I will examine the work patterns of three generations of "ordinary" college graduates, focusing first on their employment and life cycle patterns and then on their occupations.[7] The surveys reveal that higher education has had a distinctly vocational impact for women. Despite generational differences in marriage and fertility rates, alumnae of all generations entered the labor force in overwhelming numbers. What changed was the timing of their work and the occupations available to them, changes with important implications for their career trajectories.

Scholars have been critical of the influence of institutions of higher education on alumnae work patterns. Mirroring the ongoing feminist debate about the advantages of difference or similarity, separation or integration, historians have charged institutions of higher education, on the one hand, with channeling women into the service professions—less prestigious and

[6] Important work incorporating life course analysis has been done by Richard M. Bernard and Maris A. Vinovskis, "The Female School Teacher in Ante-Bellum Massachusetts," *Journal of Social History* 10 (March 1977): 332–45; Louise A. Tilly and Joan W. Scott, *Women, Work, and Family* (New York: Holt, Rinehart, Winston, 1978); and Tamara K. Hareven, *Transitions: The Family and the Life Course in Historical Perspective* (New York: Academic Press, 1978).

[7] I recognize the difficulty of defining a "generation" with any degree of precision, but for the purposes of this analysis I have divided alumnae into three large groupings, those who were graduated from about 1875–1910, 1910–1935, and 1935–1955.

less well paid than male-dominated professions—and, on the other, with imitating their male counterparts, a criticism that has applied mainly to the women's colleges.[8] The assumptions are that there exists a clear and direct relationship between higher education and what happens after and that colleges are accountable for a good deal of the later successes and failures of their graduates. But higher education alone cannot account for all differences in work patterns between college and non-college woman or for changes over time. It is a necessary rather than a sufficient condition.

I

The alumnae surveys point to one basic conclusion: Higher education for women has from the start been linked to enhanced vocational opportunity. This has also been the case for men, for whom college traditionally provided a route to the professions—initially the ministry, law, and medicine, careers that guaranteed them higher status and, usually, greater remuneration as well.[9] As higher education opened to women in the late nineteenth century, they, too, gained access to the professions, although for the most part to the feminized service professions. Higher education did not enable women to compete for jobs on equal terms with men or give them access to

[8] For the first approach, see Jill K. Conway, "Perspectives on the History of Women's Education in the United States," *History of Education Quarterly* 14 (Spring 1974): 1–12, and Frankfort, *Collegiate Women*; for the second, Joyce Antler, *The Educated Woman and Professionalization: The Struggle for a New Feminine Identity, 1890–1920* (New York: Garland Publishing, 1987), and Mabel Louise Robinson, *The Curriculum of the Woman's College*, U.S. Bureau of Education, Bulletin No. 6 (Washington, D.C.: Government Printing Office, 1918).

[9] See David F. Allmendinger, Jr., *Paupers and Scholars: The Transformation of Student Life in Nineteenth-Century New England* (New York: St Martin's Press, 1975), and Colin B. Burke, *American Collegiate Populations: A Test of the Traditional View* (New York: New York University Press, 1982).

the same jobs (or salaries). In contrast with the wide diversity of occupations available to men, women's choices have always been restricted. Although the fields open to women have expanded during the past century, gender hierachies remain in force; most women still work in sex-segregated professions, in low-paying jobs.[10]

In the nineteenth and twentieth centuries alike, college-educated women have entered the labor force more often than those with less education, while women with graduate or professional training have worked in even greater proportion.[11] The vocational impact of college was probably most marked

[10] See Joan Jacobs Brumberg and Nancy Tomes, "Women in the Professions: A Research Agenda for American Historians," *Reviews in American History* 10 (June 1982): 275–96; Cynthia Fuchs Epstein, *Woman's Place: Options and Limits in Professional Careers* (Berkeley and Los Angeles: University of California Press, 1970); Penina Migdal Glazer and Miriam Slater, *Unequal Colleagues: The Entrance of Women into the Professions, 1890–1940* (New Brunswick, N.J.: Rutgers University Press, 1987); Valerie Kincaide Oppenheimer, *The Female Labor Force in the United States: Demographic and Economic Factors Governing Its Growth and Changing Composition*, Population Monograph Series, No. 5 (Berkeley: University of California Press, 1970); and Amitai Etzioni, ed., *The Semi-Professions and Their Organization: Teachers, Nurses, Social Workers* (New York: Free Press, 1969). The use of the designation *semi-professions* for fields in which women have predominated not only reifies the mystique of the professions but obscures the real importance of gender in the development of professional hierarchies. I will use the term *profession* for vocations designated as such by the census.

[11] For the nineteenth century, see Anne Firor Scott, "The Ever Widening Circle: The Diffusion of Feminist Values from the Troy Female Seminary, 1822–1872," *History of Education Quarterly* 19 (Spring 1979): esp. 15–19; David F. Allmendinger, Jr., "Mount Holyoke Students Encounter the Need for Life-Planning, 1837–1850," *History of Education Quarterly* 19 (Spring 1979): 27–46; and Barbara Kuhn Campbell, *The "Liberated" Woman of 1914: Prominent Women in the Progressive Era* (N.p.: N.P., 1979): esp. 39–41. For the twentieth century, see, for example, National Manpower Council, *Womanpower* (New York: Columbia University Press, 1957): 74–77, and Robert W. Smuts, *Women and Work in America* (New York: Columbia University Press, 1959): 64–66. The higher employment rate for educated women seems to belie the conventional wisdom that it is principally economic need that propels women into the labor force. Explanations for the phenomenon include the skewed demographic pattern of college-educated women (who have traditionally married less often and had fewer children) and the higher salaries they command. Education is, of course, only one of several variables affecting women's work. A useful recent survey is Linda J. Waite, "U.S. Women at Work," *Population Bulletin* 36 (May 1981).

for the pioneer "first generation," which attended college in the late nineteenth century and left an unparalleled record of achievement in the professions and social reform.[12] It was the unusual woman who attended college then. In 1870 less than 2 percent of the "college-age" population, male or female, did so; in 1900, between 3 and 5 percent.[13] Such students constituted an elite, but it was an intellectual rather than a purely socioeconomic elite. The most important variable in determining who went to college was probably the educational level— or at least aspiration—of the parents, rather than their bank accounts or social pedigrees. Few women of the upper classes went to college at this time.[14]

Undoubtedly there was considerable diversity in background among students attending the nation's varied institutions of higher learning, which included land-grant universities, black colleges, and, after 1900, Catholic women's colleges. The available evidence suggests that women students came from the full range of the middle classes, including farm families, and that a major reason for attending college was preparation for a career or, at a time of imbalanced sex ratios in the Northeast, at least as a means of self-support.[15] Even for women

[12] Since women had been receiving bachelor's degrees since 1841, those who were graduated in the late nineteenth century were not the "first." Only after the Civil War, however, did women attend college in sufficient number to attain high visibility and group coherence. They identified themselves as pioneers and often spoke of themselves as a special generation.

[13] Patricia Albjerg Graham, "Expansion and Exclusion: A History of Women in American Higher Education," *Signs* 3 (Summer 1978): 759–73. Statistical estimates vary somewhat; see *Digest of Educational Statistics* (1973): 75, Burke, *American Collegiate Populations*: 215–218, and Colin B. Burke, "The Expansion of American Higher Education," in *The Transformation of Higher Learning, 1860–1930,* ed. Konrad H. Jarausch (Chicago: University of Chicago Press, 1983): 111.

[14] The educational level of mothers may have been of particular importance. For the twentieth century, see Ernest Havemann and Patricia Salter West, *They Went to College: The College Graduate in America Today* (New York: Harcourt Brace, 1954): 14–15; for an earlier period, see Allmendinger, "Mount Holyoke Students": 32, 35. Allmendinger also found a preponderance of professional fathers (and families with a surplus of daughters).

[15] On the social class and age of early women students, see Allmendinger, "Mount

from prominent families, like M. Carey Thomas, an 1877 Cornell graduate who considered most of her female peers beneath her in "social station," the motive of self-support— and the independence that went with it—was strong. A self-conscious feminist from an early age, Thomas at fourteen confided to her diary: "My, I intend to study my Classics and Mathematics next year, because I do so want to finish at Vassar and then come to Philadelphia and study for a doctor. I can't stand being dependent on anybody, even mother and father, and I want to do something besides eating, reading and dressing."[16]

In the twentieth century college attendance became a more frequent experience for both sexes.[17] After slowly rising to about

Holyoke Students": 27–46, and his "History and the Usefulness of Women's Education," *History of Education Quarterly* 19 (Spring 1979): 117–24; Sarah H. Gordon, "Smith College Students: The first Ten Classes, 1879–1888," *History of Education Quarterly* 15 (Summer 1975): 147–67; Tiziana Rota, "Between 'True Women' and 'New Women': Mount Holyoke Students, 1837 to 1908," (Ph.D. diss., University of Massachusetts, 1983): esp. 66–107; Sally Schwager, " 'Harvard Women': A History of the Founding of Radcliffe College" (Ed.D. diss., Graduate School of Education, Harvard University, 1982): esp. 234–61; Gail Apperson Kilman, "Southern Collegiate Women: Higher Education at Wesleyan Female College and Randolph-Macon Woman's College, 1893–1907," (Ph.D. diss., University of Delaware, 1984): 115–16; and Solomon, *In the Company:* 70.

[16]Marjorie Housepian Dobkin, ed., *The Making of a Feminist: Early Journals and Letters of M. Carey Thomas* (Kent, Ohio: Kent State University Press, 1979): 117, 55. See also Barbara Sicherman, *Alice Hamilton: A Life in Letters* (Cambridge, Mass.: Harvard University Press, 1984); Patricia Palmieri, "In Adamless Eden: A Social Portrait of the Academic Community at Wellesley College, 1875–1920" (Ed.D. diss., Graduate School of Education, Harvard University, 1981), and "Here Was Fellowship: A Social Portrait of Academic Women at Wellesley College, 1895–1920," *History of Education Quarterly* 23 (Summer 1983): 195–214. For an analysis of the career crises of the first generation, see Joyce Antler, " 'After College, What?': New Graduates and the Family Claim," *American Quarterly* 32 (Fall 1980): 409–34.

[17]Once begun, the entry of women into higher education proceeded rapidly: By 1900 women constituted an estimated 40 percent of all undergraduates if normal schools are included. Burke, *American Collegiate Populations:* 215–18. The rising social class of students after about 1910 is emphasized by Allmendinger, "History and the Usefulness of Women's Education": 122–23; Horowitz, *Alma Mater:* 147–51; and Solomon, *In the Company:* 71. On college youth culture, see Paula S. Fass, *The Damned and the Beautiful: American Youth in the 1920s* (New York: Oxford University Press, 1977).

15 percent of the "college-age" population by 1940, total college enrollment increased rapidly after World War II. By 1960 between a quarter and a third of the eighteen- to twenty-one-year-old group attended, while today there is 50 percent attendance, with women constituting slightly more than half of all undergraduates.[18] For the second and third generations work was a less dominant motive than it had been for Carey Thomas; it was rather one of several life objectives, something many now hoped to combine with marriage and motherhood.[19]

Yet in the twentieth century, too, the vast majority of college women have worked for some portion of their lives. Exact statistics are difficult to come by, and information is skewed to the elite, record-keeping women's colleges; but the evidence points to even higher employment rates among later generations. The largest, and most often cited, of the early surveys, a 1915 census of almost 17,000 alumnae (from the Seven Sisters, Wells College, and coeducational Cornell) found that nearly 70 percent had been gainfully employed, while a survey of some 6,600 women who attended land-grant universities between 1889 and 1922 revealed that nearly 55 percent were working in the late 1920s and that almost 82 percent had worked at some time. (Most significantly, 20 percent of the married women were currently employed, compared with 9 percent of married women in the general population.) In a recent longitudinal study, Pamela Perun and Janet Giele found that in all cohorts of students who graduated from Wellesley College between 1911 and 1960, roughly 90 percent worked at some time during their lives, with a high of 95 percent for the 1941–1945 wartime graduates.[20]

---

[18] *Digest of Educational Statistics* (1973): 75; Barbara Heyns and Joyce Adair Bird, "Recent Trends in the Higher Education of Women," in Perun, *The Undergraduate Woman*: 44–46. Figures on the 1960s vary.

[19] Work did remain an objective; even in the late 1950s 77 percent of the women (compared with 92 percent of the men) listed vocation as their primary reason for attending college. National Manpower Council, *Womanpower*: 195.

[20] Mary Van Kleeck, "A Census of College Women," *Journal of the Association of*

Although later generations seem to have worked somewhat more often than their predecessors, they did so at different stages of the life cycle. The situation may be summed up as follows: Late-nineteenth-century alumnae worked after college until they married—if they married. Women who graduated in the early and mid-twentieth century worked after marriage as well, but before they had children or after their children were grown. The implications of changing employment trends become apparent when examined in conjunction with the dramatic demographic shifts among college-educated women, who went from a pattern of high rates of singlehood, late marriage, and low fertility in the late nineteenth century to one of high marriage rates at early ages, combined with high fertility, by the mid-twentieth.[21]

The high employment rate of first-generation alumnae was due to their penchant for remaining single.[22] In view of the

Collegiate Alumnae 11 (May 1918): esp. 560; Chase Going Woodhouse, *After College—What?*, Institute of Women's Professional Relations, Bulletin No. 4 (Greensboro, N.C.: North Carolina College for Women, 1932): esp. 5, 97; Pamela J. Perun and Janet Z. Giele, "Life After College: Historical Links Between Women's Education and Women's Work," in Perun, *The Undergraduate Woman*: esp. 386–87. Other studies that reveal high proportions of working alumnae are Rota, "Between 'True Women' and 'New Women' ": esp. 246–82; Kilman, "Southern Collegiate Women," pp. 162–67; Sally Gregory Kohlstedt, "Single-Sex Education and Leadership: The Early Years of Simmons College," *Women and Educational Leadership*, ed. Sari Knopp Biklen and Marilyn B. Brannigan (Lexington, Mass.: Lexington Books, 1980): 93–112; and Joan G. Zimmerman, "Daughters of Main Street: Culture and the Female Community at Grinnell, 1884–1917," *Woman's Being, Woman's Place: Female Identity and Vocation in American History*, ed. Mary Kelley (Boston: G. K. Hall, 1979): 154–70. See also Solomon, *In the Company*: 126–28.

[21] Three articles by Mary E. Cookingham provide the fullest confirmation of the line of argument developed here: "Bluestockings, Spinsters and Pedagogues: Women College Graduates, 1865–1910," *Population Studies* 38 (November 1984): 349–64; "Combining Marriage, Motherhood, and Jobs Before World War II: Women College Graduates, Classes of 1905–1935," *Journal of Family History* 9 (Summer 1984): 178–95; and "Working After Childbearing in Modern America," *Journal of Interdisciplinary History* XIV (Spring 1984): 773–92. See also Waite, "U.S. Women at Work": esp. 7–9.

[22] On the declining marriage rates of college-educated women at the end of the nineteenth century, see Cookingham, "Bluestockings": 349–64, and Mabel Newcomer

sanctions against married women's employment, it is not surprising that the vast majority of early women graduates in the paid labor force were single. But many never married, a trend that seems to confirm the claim of many women of this generation that they viewed careers and marriage as alternative options. Among Mount Holyoke Seminary graduates between 1885 and 1889, for example, only 14 percent of those who entered the labor force ever married. And of alumnae responding to the nine-college survey in 1915, less than one-third of those who had ever worked were married, while of those who had never been employed, nearly three-fifths were married.[23]

Both at the time, when it gave rise to the "race suicide" scare, and later, the high rate of singlehood among college-educated women has been widely publicized but insufficiently analyzed. As a result, historians have not only overestimated the singlehood rates of the first generation but also misunderstood the connection between college attendance and marital status. Most historians claim that 60 (or even 70) percent of late-nineteenth-century alumnae never married, but a more reasonable estimate would be between 35 and 50 percent—still low by national standards, of course.[24] The 60 percent figure probably derives from the 1915 nine-college census but

and Evelyn S. Gibson, "Vital Statistics from Vassar College," *American Journal of Sociology* 29 (January 1924): 430–42. Cookingham attributes the low marriage rates to improved employment opportunities for educated women at a time of contracting "expected incomes" for middle-class men.

[23] Rota, "Between 'True Women' and 'New Women,' ": 257; Van Kleeck, "A Census of College Women,": 578. See also Woodhouse, *After College–What?*: 106–07.

[24] My estimate is based on such studies as: Cookingham, "Bluestockings": 351–52; Rota, "Between 'True Women' and 'New Women' ": 285; Mabel Newcomer and Ruth G. Hutchinson, "Occupations of Vassar Alumnae: A Statistical Summary of a Selected Group," *College Women and the Social Sciences*, ed. Herbert Elmer Mills (New York: John Day Co., 1934): esp. 311; L. D. Hartson, "The Occupations Which College Graduates Enter," *Vocational Guidance Magazine* 6 (April 1928): esp. 398; Kilman, "Southern Collegiate Women,": 153–55. Among those citing the 60 to 70 percent singlehood rate are Conway, "Perspectives on the History of Women's Education": p. 8, and Schwager, "Educating Women in America": 362.

is misleading because many of the respondents were recent
graduates who would marry someday; one analyst later calculated that among respondents who were graduated prior to 1900,
51 percent had married by 1915. Moreover, the marriage rates
of graduates of coeducational colleges may have been significantly higher than those of single sex institutions, which have
received most attention.[25]

The high celibacy rates have usually been attributed to the
fact of college attendance. Another possibility has been largely
ignored: the late age at which women attended college. Many
of the early students were in their twenties and thirties, most
of them teachers seeking to upgrade their skills. The average
of Radcliffe graduates in the 1890s, for example, was twenty-
nine, compared with twenty-one and a half in the 1920s.[26]
Thus, for some the relationship between college attendance
and singlehood may have been the reverse of the one usually
given, with many older single women being drawn to college
rather than women deciding to remain single after graduation.

After 1900, as the age of women college students fell and
the proportion of women attending gradually increased, alum-

[25] Van Kleeck, "A Census of College Women,": 577–78; the later calculation was by
Woodhouse, *After College—What?*: 54. Woodhouse also cites a 1916 study of marriage rates of women graduates of coeducational institutions that range from 52 to 73
percent, while her own study reported marriage rates of between 62 and 67 percent
among late-nineteenth-century graduates of land-grant institutions (pp. 53, 54). Hartson, "Occupations" (p. 298) gives a 60 percent marriage rate for Oberlin alumnae.
There was a general decline in marriage rates for U.S. women born in the late nineteenth century; they rose after about 1900; see Peter R. Uhlenberg, "A Study of Cohort
Life Cycles: Cohorts of Native Born Massachusetts Women, 1830–1920," *Population
Studies* 23 (November 1969): 407–20, and Peter Uhlenberg, "Cohort Variations in
Family Life Cycle Experiences of U.S. Females," *Journal of Marriage and the Family*
36 (May 1974): 284–92, and Margaret Gibbons Wilson, *The American Woman in
Transition: The Urban Influence, 1870–1920* (Westport, Conn.: Greenwood Press,
1979): 41–45.
[26] Solomon, *In the Company*: 70. See also Allmendinger, "History and the Usefulness
of Women's Education": 119; Amy Hewes, "Marital and Occupational Statistics of
Graduates of Mount Holyoke College," *Publications of the American Statistical Association*, N.S. 96 (December 1911): 783, and references in note 15.

nae marriage rates rose. By the mid-twentieth century, for the first time, they were about the same as the rates of those who did not attend college. For example, each cohort of Wellesley students from 1911 to 1945 married with greater frequency, the proportion rising from 69 percent of the 1911–1915 graduates to 90 percent of those graduating in the 1940s. The age of marriage also fell, from an average of thirty for the first cohort to twenty-two for 1956–1960 graduates.[27]

Changing cultural values made it acceptable for women to work after marriage and even motherhood—but only under prescribed circumstances.[28] Mary Cookingham found higher employment rates among married Mount Holyoke alumnae from post-1910 classes than in earlier cohorts, with nearly a third of those who had graduated between 1932 and 1934 working while married, but before they had children. Many returned to work in later years; nearly 50 percent of the married alumnae from the classes of 1922 to 1924 did so. Especially striking is the low fertility of early-twentieth-century graduates, a trend that encouraged labor force participation. The *average* number of children born to alumnae cohorts of the early twentieth century did not differ greatly from preceding classes. Since more women were marrying, they were having fewer children, and in many cases none at all; nearly one-third of *married* Mount Holyoke alumnae in the classes of 1923 to 1927 remained childless.[29]

---

[27] Perun and Giele, "Life After College": 395–88; Cookingham, "Combining Marriage, Motherhood, and Jobs": esp. 179. See also Hewes, "Marital and Occupational Statistics of Graduates of Mount Holyoke College": esp. 787.
[28] See Lynn Y. Weiner, *From Working Girl to Working Mother: The Female Labor Force in the United States, 1820–1980* (Chapel Hill, N.C.: University of North Carolina Press, 1985), and Smuts, *Women and Work in America*: 110–55. The growth of a consumer society in the early twentieth century contributed to the increased acceptability of work for married women. On this development, see Daniel Horowitz, *The Morality of Spending: Attitudes Toward the Consumer Society in America, 1875–1940* (Baltimore: Johns Hopkins University Press, 1985).
[29] Cookingham, "Combining Marriage, Motherhood, and Jobs": 180–84, attributes

For women who graduated in the mid-twentieth century, childbearing at early ages became the norm, as did larger families. About 90 percent of the two Wellesley cohorts of the 1940s had children, compared with 57 percent of the 1911–1915 cohort. The 1940s married alumnae had three children apiece, up substantially from the teens and twenties.[30] The new pattern of early marriage and motherhood made it difficult for women of the era to prepare for serious careers. Moreover, with the memory of women's wartime work still fresh, cultural authorities of every sort vigorously opposed the employment of mothers with young children. In retrospect, the implacable hostility to working mothers during the era of what Betty Friedan called the "feminine mystique" appears to represent a rearguard effort to stave off the inevitable, as had the warnings of physicians against the dire effects of higher education on women's health nearly a century before. As is well known, women of this generation worked in great numbers after completion of child rearing.[31]

The changing life cycle patterns had implications for the

the low fertility to a pattern of delayed childbearing, prompted in the 1920s (a time of rising living standards) by relatively high women's wages followed by the economic uncertainties of the depression (pp. 192–94). On the high proportion of childless marriages, see also Rota, "Between 'True Women' and 'New Women' ": 290–91; Wilson, *The American Woman in Transition:* 41–45; and National Manpower Council, *Womanpower:* 68. Cf. Perun and Giele, "Life After College": 386. During the 1920s there was considerable interest in the subject of working wives; see, for example, Anne Byrd Kennon, "College Wives Who Work," *Journal of the American Association of University Women* 20 (June 1927): 100–06; Virginia MacMakin Collier, *Marriage and Careers* (New York: Channel Book Shop, 1926); Chase Going Woodhouse, "Married College Women in Business and the Professions," *Annals of the American Academy of Political and Social Science* 143 (May 1929): 325–38; and Solomon, *In the Company:* 173–85.

[30] Perun and Giele, "Life After College": 386.

[31] For an analysis of responses to 1928 and 1944 Radcliffe College alumnae surveys on the possibilities of combining career and motherhood, see Solomon, *In the Company:* 182–85. On recent work patterns of women, see Oppenheimer, *The Female Labor Force:* esp. 6–111, 188–89; Waite, *U.S. Women at Work;* and Cookingham, "Working After Childbearing": 773–92.

length of women's working lives and therefore also for their career options. There is little systematic information about the timing of women's work for this period, but there are some suggestive clues. Tiziana Rota found that although nearly 23 percent of Mount Holyoke Seminary students of the 1880s had short careers (under five years), the average working life for the entire group was nearly twenty years, with one-quarter working for three decades or more. While the proportion of employed Mount Holyoke alumnae from classes that graduated in the 1920s seems to have increased, they probably worked on average for shorter periods than had women in earlier cohorts.[32]

In the context of changing life cycle patterns, the evolution of modern professionalism had serious consequences for educated women. When the demographic data are placed alongside what we know about the ever-lengthening and more costly training required of professionals in the twentieth century, it is clear that the odds against women's seeking demanding careers increased. The medical profession, in which women carved out a respectable place for themselves in the late nineteenth century, offers an especially interesting case. As educational standards were upgraded to include longer training both before medical school (by requiring first two and then four years of college) and afterward (by adding internships and later residencies), the proportion of women in medical schools fell. The upgrading of legal education came later but followed a similar pattern.[33] Under such circumstances, high career costs, com-

---

[32] Rota, "Between 'New Women' and 'True Women' ": esp. 264, and Cookingham, "Combining Marriage, Motherhood, and Jobs": 184–85. Newcomer and Hutchinson, "Occupations of Vassar Alumnae," also found a greater proportion of Vassar graduates from the classes of 1917–1926 working than among 1892–1901 graduates (esp. p. 313).

[33] On changes in medicine, law, and academe, see Hummer, *The Decade of Elusive Promise*. On the complex situation in medicine, see Regina Markell Morantz-Sanchez, *Sympathy and Science: Women Physicians in American Medicine* (New York: Oxford University Press, 1985); Mary Roth Walsh, *"Doctors Wanted: No Women Need Apply": Sexual Barriers in the Medical Profession, 1835–1975* (New Haven:

bined with uncertain employment prospects, may have proved prohibitive to women who, if they wanted to work, also wanted to marry and thus could not be certain about the timing or duration of their employment. As for the declining proportion of women earning doctorates in the late 1940s and 1950s, many must have been discouraged, if not by the high singlehood rates, then by the long years of training and outright discrimination; even the women's colleges hired men with greater frequency, in part to shed the negative image that spinsters were thought to project in the twentieth century.[34]

By remaining single, the early college women made choices about their lives that enabled them to have sustained and influential careers. For the long-term or lifetime worker, serious investment in a career was worthwhile. It appears likely that later generations of college women worked, on average, for shorter periods of time and in less demanding professions. As social conventions changed to permit middle-class women to work while married, their work also became less continuous, hence at a competitive disadvantage in the context of

Yale University Press, 1977); and Virginia G. Drachman, "The Limits of Progress. the Professional Lives of Women Doctors, 1881–1926," *Bulletin of the History of Medicine* 60 (Spring 1986): 58–72. Efforts to upgrade the profession led to the closing of marginal schools and an overall reduction in the number of practitioners. The change in the proportion of women in the profession was dramatic. At the University of Michigan, for example, the proportion of women medical graduates declined from 25 percent in 1890 to 3.1 percent in 1910, while at Johns Hopkins the proportion dropped from one-third in 1896 to one-tenth in 1916 (Walsh, *"Doctors Wanted"*: 205, 193). Walsh emphasizes discrimination, while Morantz-Sanchez found that applications of women schools declined in the early twentieth century and suggests that many regarded the new field of social work as an acceptable and less costly alternative (pp. 232–65).

[34] Margaret W. Rossiter, *Women Scientists in America: Struggles and Strategies to 1940* (Baltimore: Johns Hopkins University Press, 1982): 160–217, has telling data on the preference for male professors at some women's colleges as early as the 1920s. Emilie J. Hutchinson, *Women and the Ph.D.*, Institute for Women's Professional Relations, Greensboro, N.C. Bulletin No. 2 (December 1929), cites a singlehood rate of 75 percent among women who received the Ph.D. between 1877 and 1927 (p. 90).

twentieth-century professional life. Moreover, the traditional taboo against mothers with young children joining the labor force remained strong. Cultural pressures and the lack of institutional supports made it difficult for all but the hardiest women graduates of the mid-twentieth century to combine work and motherhood, at least on a full-time basis. Finally, the increased emphasis on heterosexual family life undermined the social networks and communal arrangements of the pioneers (especially those in the women's colleges and social settlements), depriving women of sources of encouragement and political strength that had sustained many through difficult work situations.

II

Although changing life course patterns undermined women's ability to prepare for high-status careers in the twentieth century, higher education for women has been correlated throughout its history with improved vocational options. The late nineteenth century was a time of expanding employment opportunities for women; the vast majority worked in domestic service and factories.[35] By contrast, college-educated women entered the new service professions and clerical work to a degree and even made progress in such traditionally male fields as medicine and academe. But although women who attended college had substantially better vocational options than their less educated sisters, their choices were not unlimited. Whether they were briefly en route to marriage or other careers or to a

---

[35] For an overview, see Alice Kessler-Harris, *Out of Work: A History of Wage-Earning Women in the United States* (New York: Oxford University Press, 1982). On black women, see the special issue on workers, *Sage* 3 (Spring 1986), and Phyllis A. Wallace, with Linda Datcher and Julianne Malveaux, *Black Women in the Labor Force* (Cambridge, Mass: Harvard University Press, 1980).

lifework, an overwhelming proportion of them engaged in just one profession—teaching.

The preponderance of teachers was particularly marked among the first generation. Teachers constituted less than 6 percent of all women workers in 1910. But among the 17,000 alumnae who answered the 1915 nine-college survey, more than four-fifths of those who had ever been gainfully employed had taught, while nearly 60 percent of all respondents had done so at some time.[36] The propensity of the early college graduates to teach is surprising only in its degree. From the early nineteenth century, when women first entered public school systems, the feminization of the teaching profession proceeded at a rapid pace. By 1870 women constituted 59 percent of the force; by 1920—an all-time peak—86 percent. (In 1978, about two-thirds of public school teachers were women.)[37]

It is no accident that the opening of colleges and universities to women after the Civil War coincided with the feminization of teaching and the introduction of compulsory education for a growing urban population. Indeed, the demand for public school teachers forced public institutions of higher learning to admit women. Some initially countenanced coeducation through the back door of a normal school, while others established education programs shortly after admitting women; by 1890 more than one hundred institutions offered pedagogy courses.[38] Even the women's colleges, despite their general

[36] Van Kleeck, "A Census of College Woman": 559–63. A large proportion of alumnae from other institutions also taught; see Zimmerman, "Daughters of Main Street": 157; Kilman, "Southern Collegiate Women": 162–64; Cynthia Horsburgh Requardt, "Alternative Professions for Goucher College Graduates, 1892–1910," *Maryland Historical Magazine* 74 (September 1979): 275; and Helen R. Olin, *The Women of a State University* (New York: N.p., 1909): 167–208.

[37] David B. Tyack, *The One Best System: A History of American Urban Education* (Cambridge, Mass.: Harvard University Press 1974): 61, and David B. Tyack and Myra H. Strober, "Jobs and Gender: A History of the Structuring of Educational Employment by Sex," *Educational Policy and Management* (New York: N.p., 1981): 133.

[38] Clifford, " 'Shaking Dangerous Questions from the Crease,' ": 22–37, and Willard

resistance to vocational education, bowed to the inevitable and, beginning in the 1890s, introduced courses in pedagogy.[39] From the start women enrolled in different courses from men. In addition to the teacher training programs, they flocked to the liberal arts, outnumbering men in these courses in many coeducational institutions by the end of the century. The trend alarmed male administrators, who saw in the statistics a kind of "Gresham's Law . . . The weaker sex drives out the stronger." Women's preference for the "culture course" also worried some female educators who viewed the liberal arts degree as impractical.[40] But even women who did not enroll in vocational courses and programs were effectively preparing themselves for care..rs in teaching. In the late nineteenth century a liberal arts degree *was* a vocational degree.[41] It guaranteed some familiarity with

S. Elsbree, *The American Teacher: Evolution of a Profession in a Democracy* (New York: American Book Company, 1939): 311–34. See also *The University of Michigan: An Encyclopedic Survey* (Ann Arbor, Mich.: 1953): 3: 1073–97; Merle Curti and Vernon Carstensen, *The University of Wisconsin, 1848–1925* (Madison, Wis.: University of Wisconsin Press, 1949): 116–120: 2: 251–57; Debra Herman, "College and After: The Vassar Experiment in Women's Education, 1981–1924" (Ph.D. diss., Stanford University, 1979): 243–53.

[39] Information from Bryn Mawr College Library, Mount Holyoke College Library, Radcliffe College Archives, Smith College Archives, Wellesley College Archieves; Herman, "College and After": 248, 278; Kilman, "Southern Collegiate Women": 162–63; and Robinson, *The Curriculum of the Woman's College*: 62–63. The tendency to teach was more marked among alumnae from some institutions than others. In 1915 some 90 percent of Mount Holyoke's working alumnae had taught. By contrast, Vassar, which did not have a pedagogy department until 1943, produced fewer teachers than its sister colleges. Rota, "Between 'True Women' and 'New Women' ": 236; Herman, "College and After": 248, 278.

[40] Quotation from Mary Roth Walsh and Francis R. Walsh, "Integrating Men's Colleges at the Turn of the Century, *Historical Journal of Massachusetts* 10 (June 1982): 11. See also Rosalind Rosenberg, *Beyond Separate Spheres: Intellectual Roots of Modern Feminism* (New Haven: Yale University Press, 1982): 43–53; Lynn D. Gordon, "Co-education on Two Campuses: Berkeley and Chicago, 1890–1912," in Kelley, *Woman's Being, Woman's Place*: 171–93; Zimmerman, "Daughters of Main Street": 157–60; and Florence Howe, *Myths of Coeducation: Selected Essays, 1964–1983* (Bloomington, Ind.: Indiana University Press, 1984): esp. 206–20. See also "Discussion of College Curricula," *Proceedings of the Association of Collegiate Alumnae* 3 (December 1898): 1–46.

[41] See Clifford, " 'Shaking Dangerous Questions from the Crease' ": 41. On the new

languages, literature, mathematics, and science, the staples of secondary school teaching.[42] Indeed, liberal arts colleges seem to have "produced" relatively more teachers than universities did, but perhaps they drew students of a different type in the first place.[43]

Before the introduction of fixed teacher training requirements, a woman who had attended college, even one who had not graduated, was a desirable addition to any school system.[44] College-educated women constituted a professional elite. Although the vast majority of teachers—including those trained in normal schools—worked in primary schools, college alumnae taught in disproportionate numbers in high schools. Secondary education had greater prestige and was also less sex-segregated (in 1905 men constituted 38 percent of high school but only 2 percent of primary school teachers). The pay was low, however, especially in the private schools, where many graduates of elite colleges taught.[45]

diversity of courses and programs available to students in the late nineteenth century, see Laurence R. Veysey, *The Emergence of the American University* (Chicago: University of Chicago Press, 1965); Frederick Rudolph, *The American College and University: A History* (New York: Knopf, 1962); and Frederick Rudolph, *Curriculum: A History of the American Undergraduate Course of Study Since 1636* (San Francisco: Jossey-Bass Publishers, 1978).

[42] A surprisingly large number of women elected science courses, presumably mainly in preparation for teaching. At Wellesley 37 percent of students graduating between 1883 and 1895 took the B.S. degree. Virginia Onderdonk, "The Curriculum," *Wellesley College, 1875–1975: A Century of Women*, ed. Jean Glasscock (Wellesley: N.p., 1975): 126–30. See also Rossiter, *Women Scientists:* 9–19, on the excellence of science education at the women's colleges.

[43] Clifford " 'Shaking Dangerous Questions from the Crease' ": 22–24. For suggestive data on career paths of students at different institutions, see Woodhouse, *After College—What?*: 18, 26–28; Kennon, "College Wives Who Work": 100–06; and Kohlstedt, "Single-Sex Education and Leadership: The Early Years of Simmons College": 93–112.

[44] The course of study at normal schools ranged from two to four years, and many required no more than a year or two of high school for entrance. Not until 1907 did the first state require a high school diploma of its teachers, and well into the twentieth century many had no more than a grammar school education. See Elsbree, *The American Teacher:* 311–34.

[45] Tyack, *The One Best System:* 61–62. On the affinity of college women for second-

What conclusions can be drawn about teaching as a profession for women? In this, as in so many aspects of women's experiences, the balance sheet is mixed. Teaching unquestionably served as a temporary livelihood for many women, permitting them to finance their educations, or to support themselves, and often other family members as well, in respectable, if not resplendent, fashion. But a career in education did not serve as a vehicle for professional mobility for women in the way that it did for men. Women had less chance of promotion within the profession since men, far in excess of their numbers, became principals and superintendents. Male educators were more likely to be found in colleges and universities and in secondary schools; for those men who taught the lower grades, teaching was often a temporary vocation before they took up their main work. Women had fewer opportunities to move on to advantageous positions in other fields. Indeed, the heavy concentration of college-educated women in this one occupation reveals the limits on women's professional aspirations. Male graduates had a much wider choice. A 1912 study revealed that in addition to education, large numbers of college-educated men entered commerce, law, medicine, the ministry, and engineering; all but medicine were virtually closed to women.[46]

ary school teaching, see Cookingham, "Combining Marriage, Motherhood, and Jobs": 185; *The Educated Woman in America*, ed. Barbara M. Cross (New York: Teachers College Press, 1965): 164; and Hewes, "Marital and Occupational Statistics": 793; on salaries, see ibid.: 796; Woodhouse, *After College—What?*: 29–52; "College Women in Non-Teaching Occupations: A Study Made by the Committee on Vocational Opportunities Other Than Teaching," *Proceedings of the Association of Collegiate Alumnae* 6 (April 1913): 73–88; and Susan M. Kingsbury, *Economic Status of University Women in the U.S.A.*, U.S. Women's Bureau Bulletin No. 170 (Washington, D.C.: Government Printing Office, 1939).

[46] David Tyack and Elisabeth Hansot, *Managers of Virtue: Public School Leadership in America, 1820–1980* (New York: Basic Books, 1982): 180–201; Burke, *American Collegiate Populations*: 189–90; Bailey B. Burritt, *Professional Distribution of College and University Graduates*, U.S. Bureau of Education, Bulletin No. 19 (Washington, D.C.: Government Printing Office, 1912). On teaching as a career, see also Nancy Hoffman, ed., *Woman's "True" Profession: Voices from the History of Teaching* (Old Westbury: Feminist Press, 1981); and Solomon, *In the Company*: 126–28.

As a projected lifework, therefore, teaching often seemed like a dead end to an ambitious woman. As Grace Abbott, who had tried it, later observed, "A boy can come home from college, begin the practice of his profession, and advance rapidly in his home town. But when a girl comes back, what can she do? She can teach, but after she's done that she finds that she has reached the top, that there is nothing more for her." (Abbott followed her older sister, Edith, to graduate school and had a distinguished career in social work.)[47] Careers in education also placed severe constraints on the personal lives of women and in the late nineteenth century precluded marriage. Even in the twentieth century married women were long the victims of outright discrimination. A 1931 survey of 1,500 school systems, for example, revealed that 77 percent refused to hire married women while 63 percent dismissed women teachers who later married. The salaries of married women teachers were also lower than those of their single colleagues.[48]

Teaching was a vehicle of upward mobility for second-generation Irish-American and Jewish women. The former entered the public school systems of large cities in the late nineteenth century. By the first decade of the twentieth century they constituted the largest group of teachers in New York City and a large proportion of the urban teaching force elsewhere. It is likely that many attended normal schools or teachers colleges and, after 1900, the new Catholic women's colleges. Many Irish teachers were nuns, a likely reason that the marriage rates of educated Catholic women remained low well into the twentieth century.[49] Second-generation Jewish women entered

[47] Lela B. Costin, *Two Sisters for Social Justice: A Biography of Grace and Edith Abbott* (Urbana and Chicago: University of Illinois Press, 1983): 24.
[48] Ruth Shallcross, *Should Married Women Work?* (Washington, D.C.: Public Affairs Committee, 1940): 7. See also Chase Going Woodhouse, "May Married Women Teach?," *Journal of the American Association of University Women* 25 (April 1932): 140–45; Scharf, *To Work and to Wed*: 66–85.
[49] On Irish teachers, see Hasia R. Diner, *Erin's Daughters in America: Irish Immigrant Women in the Nineteenth Century* (Baltimore: John Hopkins University Press, 1983): 97–98; Clifford, " 'Marry, Stitch, Die, or Do Worse' "; 252–53; and Mary J.

teaching in large number after World War I; between 1920 and 1940 the proportion of Jews among new public school teachers in New York City increased from 26 to 56 percent. Many of the women received free educations at Brooklyn and Hunter colleges.[50]

For black women, careers in education offered relatively more promising opportunities than they did for white women, a reflection of inferior status of blacks in American society. Teaching was virtually the only profession open to black women well into the twentieth century. Even nursing and clerical work were long closed to them, and many black families made substantial sacrifices to secure the necessary training so their daughters could avoid the most frequent alternative—domestic service. Teaching was such an important career for black women, and professional opportunities for black men so limited, that in the 1940s more women than men received degrees

Oates, "The Professional Preparation of Parochial School Teachers 1870–1940," *Historical Journal of Massachusetts* 12 (January 1984): 60–72. Marriage rates by religion are given in Havemann and West, *They Went to College:* 55. Catholic higher education for women is a virtually untouched subject, but the introduction to Mary J. Oates, ed., *Higher Education for Catholic Women: An Historical Anthology* (New York: Garland Publishing, 1987), is a fine start. See also Solomon, *In the Company.*: 144–46, 153–56, and Theresa A. Rector, "Black Nuns as Educators," *Journal of Negro Education* 51 (Summer 1982): 238–53.

[50] Deborah Dash Moore, *At Home in America: Second Generation New York Jews* (New York: Columbia University Press, 1981): 95–99; Ruth Jacknow Markowitz, "The Daughters of Immigrants as College Students: Their Role as Student Activists During the 1930s," unpublished paper presented at the Organization of American Historians, 1986: 2–5. Access to local education is an important variable in women's vocational options. The opening up of municipal institutions, such as Brooklyn and Hunter Colleges, or those that drew mainly on a local clientele, such as Temple University in Philadelphia, helped many women (who often took second place to their brothers when family resources were scarce) to attain low-cost educations. Richard Angelo found more women and blacks, as well as more working-class and foreign-born individuals, attending Temple than the University of Pennsylvania, where tuition was nearly double. Among Protestant students who received degrees from Temple between 1926 and 1935, 40 percent were enrolled in the education program. See "The Social Transformation of American Higher Education," in Jarausch, *The Transformation of Higher Learning, 1860–1930:* esp. 286–90.

from black colleges. A decade later nearly two-thirds of the bachelor's degrees granted by black colleges went to women; by contrast, some two-thirds of the graduates of nonblack colleges in the 1950s were men.[51]

The occupations of college-educated women diversified in the twentieth century, as did those of women professionals generally. In 1870 teachers and college educators constituted 90 percent of all women classified by the census as professionals; only two other fields, nursing and music, employed as much as 1 percent of women in the professional category. By 1940 the proportion in education had declined to 55 percent, while nurses constituted nearly one-quarter of all professional women. Seven other occupations acccounted for 1 percent or more of the total. In order of importance they were: social and religious workers, musicians and music teachers, librarians and library attendants, artists and art teachers, doctors and medical service workers, and editors and reporters.[52]

[51] Jeanne L. Noble, *The Negro Woman's College Education* (New York: Teachers College, Columbia University, 1956): esp. 28–31; Linda M. Perkins, "The Education of Black Women: A Historical Perspective," unpublished paper presented at the Organization of American Historians, April 1984: esp. 19; Marion Vera Cuthbert, *Education and Marginality: A Study of the Negro Woman College Graduate* (New York: Stratford Press, 1942); Mamie Garvin Fields, with Karen Fields, *Lemon Swamp and Other Places: A Carolina Memoir* (New York: Free Press, 1983); "Black Women in Education," special issue, *Journal of Negro Education* 51 (Summer 1982), esp. Sharon Harley, "Beyond the Classroom: The Organizational Lives of Black Female Educators in the District of Columbia, 1890–1930": 254–65; and Solomon, *In the Company:* 128, 151–53.

[52] Janet M. Hooks, *Women's Occupations Through Seven Decades*, U.S. Women's Bureau, Bulletin No. 218 (Washington, D.C.: Government Printing Office, 1951): 155–79. See also Rudolph C. Blitz, "Women in the Professions, 1870–1970," *Monthly Labor Review* 97 (May 1974): 34–39; Joseph A. Hill, *Women in Gainful Occupations, 1870 to 1920*, U.S. Bureau of the Census, Census Monographs 9 (Washington, D.C.: Government Printing Office, 1929); and Elizabeth Kemper Adams, *Women Professional Workers* (New York: N.p., 1921). In view of the relative importance of music as a field of employment for women, the early introduction of music courses at the women's colleges may well have had more of a vocational impact than has been recognized. On the Wellesley program, which included a major, see Onderdonk, "The Curriculum": 132–34, 142–43.

Colleges and universities trained students for most of these professions. The exception was nursing. The second largest but probably the least prestigious women's profession, nursing was near the bottom of the list of occupations for college women in the 1915 alumnae survey, outranked by both medicine and science. Granted that respondents came mainly from liberal arts colleges that drew students from relatively privileged socio-economic backgrounds, it is also true that until recently most nurse training programs were hospital- rather than university-based. By the mid-1920s twenty-five academic institutions granted bachelor's degrees in nursing, but enrollments were small. As late as 1962 only 14 percent of all nurses were graduated from baccalaureate programs.[53]

By contrast, librarianship and home economics did draw college women, although not equally from all types of institutions. Home economics, a new field in the 1890s, was taught at more than one hundred academic institutions by 1910. At Cornell and other land-grant universities, it was a popular major for women, many of whom later entered teaching. The subject made few inroads at liberal arts colleges. Vassar established a widely publicized "euthenics program," an undergraduate home economics course introduced in the mid-1920s. But although it survived until the late 1950s, the program drew few students.[54]

---

[53] Philip A. Kalisch and Beatrice J. Kalisch, *The Advance of American Nursing* (Boston: Little, Brown, 1978): esp. 337–41, 602–05, 624–26; Barbara Melosh, *"The Physician's Hand": Work Culture and Conflict in American Nursing* (Philadelphia: Temple University Press, 1982), pp. 207–08. Six years after Radcliffe had instituted a combined liberal arts and nursing program in 1945, only fifteen individuals (one-third of those entering) had completed it, while twenty-three had dropped out after receiving their bachelor's degrees. See Everett Cherrington Hughes, "Report of a Study of the Coordinated Program of Radcliffe College and the Massachusetts General Hospital School of Nursing and of Its Broader Implications," Radcliffe College Archives. On black nurses, see Darlene Clark Hine, "From Hospital to College: Black Nurse Leaders and the Rise of Collegiate Nursing Schools," *Journal of Negro Education* 51 (Summer 1982): 22–237, and Julianne Malveaux and Susan Englander, "Race and Class in Nursing Occupations," *Sage* 3 (Spring 1986): 41–45.

[54] On librarianship, see Dee Garrison, *Apostles of Culture: The Public Librarian and*

In the teens and twenties the fastest-growing fields for college women were social service and business. In the latter category many positions were stenographic or clerical, fields encouraged by the new vocational bureaus established by some colleges. Typing was already a desirable asset for college women; one who had gone into editorial work noted in 1913 that a course in stenography "helped me more in getting a start than all the college courses put together." If we assume that some women accepted secretarial positions as their only entrée into the publishing and commercial worlds, it is still a comment on the changing nature of college women's ambitions—as well as their possibilities—that so many of the second generation chose secretarial and clerical work. It is also a comment on the poor pay of teachers.[55]

For twentieth-century alumnae, social service offered an attractive alternative to teaching and one more prestigious than nursing or business. It was also probably the only profession that offered significant opportunities for leadership to both women and men. A new profession that grew out of women's earlier voluntary activities, social work was the second most frequent occupation reported in the 1915 alumnae survey and by 1940 the third-largest census category for professional women. The field provides one of the clearest links between extracurricular collegiate life and later activities, if not always long-term career choice. Indeed, it seems to have been one of the

American Society, 1876–1920 (New York: Free Press, 1979); on home economics, Emma Seifrit Weigley, "It Might Have Been Euthenics: The Lake Placid Conferences and the Home Economics Movement," *American Quarterly* 26 (March 1974): 79–96; Antler, *The Educated Woman and Professionalization:* 91–97. On Vassar, see Herman, "College and After": 312–31, and Horowitz, *Alma Mater:* 295–302; on Cornell, Charlotte Williams Conable, *Women at Cornell: The Myth of Equal Education* (Ithaca, N.Y.: Cornell University Press, 1977). Smith's more innovative Institute for the Coordination of Women's Interests, which combined research with cooperative nursery and kitchen ventures, lasted only six years. See Dolores Hayden, *The Grand Domestic Revolution: A History of Feminist Designs for American Homes, Neighborhoods, and Cities* (Cambridge, Mass.: MIT Press, 1981): 271–77.
[55] See "College Women in Non-Teaching Occupations": 73–88, and Herman, "College and After": 279–81.

few fields that the women's colleges deliberately fostered, perhaps because it still hovered between the vocational and the avocational and also comported with traditional notions of noblesse oblige and women's presumed moral mission. College clubs had links with such organizations as the YWCA, the Charity Organization Society, and the College Settlements Association (CSA). At Goucher College, where the campus clubs were strong, more than 14 percent of the graduating classes of 1892–1910 entered social work. The CSA, founded in 1890 by representatives of several women's colleges, built student participation into its organizational structure; each member college had one alumna and one undergraduate board member. Students took part in settlement activities, sometimes in connection with a course in economics or sociology, new fields in the 1890s that attracted many women students. The three institutions that provided the most support for the CSA—Wellesley, Smith, and Vassar—also sent the most women into settlement work. [56]

Women who went to college in the twentieth century had a greater vocational choice than their predecessors. [57] Never-

[56] See Requardt, "Alternative Professions for Goucher College Graduates": 275, 277–79; College Settlements Association, *Annual Reports*, 1890–1900; John P. Rousmaniere, "Cultural Hybrid in the Slums: The College Woman and the Settlement House, 1889–1894," *American Quarterly* 22 (Spring 1970): 45–66. A useful recent overview is Clarke A. Chambers, "Women in the Creation of the Profession of Social Work," *Social Service Review* 60 (March 1986): 1–33. See also Allen F. Davis, *Spearheads for Reform: The Social Settlements and the Progressive Movement, 1890–1914* (New York: Oxford University Press, 1967), and Roy Lubove, *The Professional Altruist: The Emergence of Social Work As a Career, 1880–1930* (Cambridge, Mass.: Harvard University Press, 1965). On the popularity of the social sciences, see Mills, *College Women and the Social Sciences*, and Zimmerman, "Daughters of Main Street": 157.

[57] Around 1910 educators concerned about the vocational prospects of alumnae, especially the disproportionate number that entered teaching, established employment bureaus and in other ways also tried to promote women's vocational opportunities. See Antler, *The Educated Women and Professionalization*: 84–90. The 1915 nine-college survey of nearly 17,000 alumnae reported that with each passing decade relatively more women took up work fields other than teaching, a finding supported by other studies as well. Van Kleeck, "A Census of College Women": 561–67.

theless, as late as 1948, more than half the respondents to an American Association of University Women (AAUW) survey were teachers.[58] Women still enrolled in different courses and prepared for different professions from men. In 1955 about half the women receiving bachelor's and first professional degrees did so in education, nursing, library science, and home economics; nearly two-thirds received degrees in these fields and in English and fine arts.[59]

III

Now that we have examined long-term trends in marriage and labor force participation, what generalizations can be made about the relationship between college and later vocation?[60]

The links between higher education and women's work experiences are neither obvious nor direct. The relative impact

[58] Patricia Woodward Cautley, AAUW *Members Look at College Education: An Interim Report* (N.p.: N.p., 1948), p. 5. See also Herman, "College and After": pp. 278–79.
[59] National Manpower Council, *Womanpower*. 201–03. See also Michelle Patterson, "Sex and Specialization in Academe and the Professions," *Academic Women on the Move*, ed. Alice S. Rossi and Ann Calderwood (New York: Russell Sage Foundation, 1973): 313–31; Saul D. Feldman, *Escape from the Doll's House: Women in Graduate and Professional School Education* (New York: McGraw-Hill, 1974): 37–75; Heyns and Bird, "Recent Trends in the Higher Education of Women": 50–51.
[60] Research needs to be done on this subject. The information currently available is not only scanty but skewed to the women's colleges (and, among them, the Seven Sisters), which in the twentieth century have educated only a small proportion of all women. These colleges have traditionally emphasized the liberal arts rather than the more overtly vocational programs that flourished at public institutions and some private universities as well. Yet they turned out large numbers of professionals, including many who entered nontraditional fields. Obviously a liberal arts major does not by itself lead to a career in medicine, law, or librarianship. In the twentieth century postgraduate education has been a prerequisite for most professions, but even earlier many college women sought additional training. See, for example, Perun and Giele, "Life After College": 386; Rota, "Between 'True Women' and 'New Women' ": esp. 238–45; Sophia Meranski, "A Census of Mount Holyoke College Alumnae." *Alumnae Quarterly* (October 1924): 149–50.

of advanced education must be weighed against such factors as individual preference and prior educational experience as well as the socioeconomic status, cultural background, and psychological impact of particular families—all of which social scientists have identified as crucial to the decision to attend college in the first place. Moreover, it is difficult to measure the direct effects of the curriculum against extracurricular activities, peer pressures, the turmoil of adolescence, and cultural norms concerning female behavior. Finally, there is the impact of long-range historical and economic trends, including wars, business cycles, and changing occupational structures. In other words, *after* college does not necessarily mean *because of* college.

The ongoing controversy about which institutions are likely to "produce" the most scholars or otherwise notable women indicates the difficulty of generalizing about the relationship between institutional choice and vocational outcome. The subject of women in science—the ultimate "male" field—has been the most hotly debated. Recently Mary Oates and Susan Williamson, challenging earlier studies by M. Elizabeth Tidball and Vera Kistiakowsky, have maintained that it is not women's colleges per se but only the elite Seven Sisters that "produced" distinguished graduates at a higher rate than small coeducational colleges, a result they attribute to the greater selectivity of the Seven Sisters and, even more, to the higher socioeconomic background of the students. Earlier Mabel Newcomer also maintained that the success of women's college graduates had more to do with the students themselves than with the quality of the education they received, surely a discouraging admission by a longtime Vassar professor.[61]

[61] See M. Elizabeth Tidball and Vera Kistiakowsky, "Baccalaureate Origins of American Scientists and Scholars," *Science* 193 (1976): 646–52; Rossiter, *Women Scientists:* 144–52; Mary J. Oates and Susan Williamson, "Women's Colleges and Women Achievers," *Signs* 3 (1978): 795–806; M. Elizabeth Tidball, "Women's Colleges and Women Achievers Revisited," *Signs* 5 (1980): 504–17; Newcomer, *A Century of Higher Education:* 128.

Janet Giele's recent study of alumnae (classes of 1934–1979) from two selective institutions, coeducational Oberlin and one of the Seven Sisters (whose identity was kept confidential), further highlights the problem of sorting out the impact of educational experience from socioeconomic and family background. She finds some differences in alumnae profiles: More of the graduates of the women's college went into "nontraditional" fields, while more of the Oberlin alumnae were working at the time of the study and had graduate training. But Giele also notes subtle differences in occupational profiles of the families of the two groups, of which perhaps the most interesting is that the mothers of the Oberlin students were better educated and more likely to work than those of their women's college counterpart.[62]

Some colleges do develop reputations for turning out specialists in specific fields. In such cases students may be drawn to an institution because of matching interests or may be turned on by the quality of a program, or both. Mount Holyoke, for example, which nurtured teachers (the most traditional work for college women), also fostered more than its share of scientists. Both the zoology and the chemistry departments had national reputations, while the group research project initiated by chemistry professor Emma Perry Carr was a model of the kind of environment that can stimulate students in a particular direction. Alumnae of Barnard College, which was unusual in having an undergraduate anthropology department, made a strong showing in that field, while graduates of Bryn Mawr and Vassar were more apt to choose, respectively, careers in geology and psychology.[63]

---

[62] Perhaps surprisingly, Oberlin alumnae also married less often and had fewer children. Janet Zollinger Giele, "Coeducation or Women's Education? A Comparison of Alumnae from Two Colleges: 1934–79," *Educating Women and Men Together: Coeducation in a Changing World*, ed. Carol Lasser and Sandra J. Peacock (Urbana, Ill.: University of Illinois Press, 1987).

[63] Rossiter, *Women Scientists*: 144–52; Meranski, "A Census of Mount Holyoke College Alumnae": 149–59; Martha H. Verbrugge, "Emma Perry Carr," in *Notable*

In addition to formal education and family background, national events and public policy have influenced women's vocational options, although often only for specific cohorts. During World War I, for example, more college women entered nursing than usual. Many studied at the newly established Training Camp for Nurses at Vassar which recruited more than 400 alumnae from 115 institutions. But the influx of college women into nursing was short-lived and the numbers dropped off sharply after the war. The shortage of men on the home front during the war prompted the admission of women to the Yale and Columbia medical schools and also gave women physicians access to several prestigious internships for the first time. But these changes did not significantly alter the long-range decline of women in medicine.[64]

The depression and World War II also affected the employment opportunities of specific cohorts of women, but their lasting consequences are still debated by historians. During the depression the proportion of women in teaching, social work, and librarianship declined. Clearly jobs in these fields became more attractive to men when other work was scarce. In addition, married women teachers were pushed out of the labor

American Women: The Modern Period, ed. Barbara Sicherman and Carol Hurd Green (Cambridge, Mass.: Harvard University Press, 1980): 136–38, and articles on biologists, chemists, anthropologists, geologists, and psychologists in the same volume, as well as those in Edward T. James, Janet Wilson James, and Paul S. Boyer, eds., *Notable American Women, 1607–1950* (Cambridge, Mass.: Harvard University Press, 1971), 3 vols.
[64] Kalisch and Kalisch, *The Advance of American Nursing*: 295–312; Gladys Bonner Clappison, *Vassar's Rainbow Division: The Training Camp for Nurses at Vassar College* (Lake Mills, Iowa: Graphic Publishing, 1964); *One Hundred Year Biographical Directory of Mount Holyoke College, 1837–1937* (South Hadley, Mass.: N.p., 1937): 706. Although many of the Vassar-trained nurses dropped out after the armistice, those who continued constituted a professional elite. The government established the Army School of Nursing, and the wartime appeal also increased applications to regular nursing schools. But these efforts did not survive the war, and by 1920 there was an acute shortage of nurses. On the situation of women doctors, see Walsh, "*Doctors Wanted*": 207–35, and Morantz-Sanchez, *Sympathy and Science*: 232–65, 312–50.

force; in 1930, for example, fewer school districts hired married women than had done so three years before.[65]

World War II has often been considered a major catalyst for the subsequent increase of women in the labor force. But recently scholars have suggested that significant numbers of married women were entering the labor force in the 1930s, while economists view the rapid growth of the feminized service fields rather than the war as the most important factor in the rise in female employment in the 1950s. Nor did the war alter attitudes toward women's work: After Rosie the Riveter came the feminine mystique.[66] The aftermath of the war did, however, contribute to the falling proportion of women attaining bachelor's degrees. The decline was not a matter of diminished female aspiration but of the largess, in the form of the GI Bill of Rights, that made it possible for World War II veterans to attend college. By covering married veterans, the law also encouraged early marriage, thereby adversely affecting, at least in the short run, the educational and career prospects of many women.[67]

Did higher education make a difference for women? Certainly it did. In addition to the oft-cited personal testimony of the pioneer generation are the quantitative data that have been presented here. It is apparent that college permitted women,

[65] Scharf, *To Work and to Wed:* esp. 66–103; Sticker, "Cookbooks, and Law Books"; and Susan Ware, *Holding Their Own: American Women in the 1930s* (Boston: Twayne, 1982): esp. 76–77. The proportion of men in teaching later declined, but not before many had established themselves in administrative positions.

[66] Chafe, *The American Woman:* 135–95; Karen Anderson, *Wartime Women: Sex Roles, Family Relations, and the Status of Women During World War II* (Westport, Conn.: Greenwood Press, 1981); Susan M. Hartmann, *The Home Front and Beyond: American Women in the 1940s* (Boston: Twayne, 1982): esp. 77–99; Maureen Honey, *Creating Rosie the Riveter: Class, Gender, and Propaganda During World War II* (Amherst, Mass.: University of Massachusetts Press, 1984): 1–17; D'Ann Campbell, *Women at War with America: Private Lives in a Patriotic Era* (Cambridge, Mass.: Harvard University Press, 1984). Oppenheimer, *The Female Labor Force*, emphasizes segmented labor markets.

[67] Hartmann, *The Home Front:* 25–26, 105–07.

both those committed to careers and those who entered the labor force in more discontinuous fashions, to work in professional capacities. Indeed, for whatever reason—whether because of reduced marriage and fertility or because early employment fosters a greater desire for work or financial independence—college women were more likely to work at all ages and thus, perhaps, also to experience the increase in authority that usually comes to women who contribute to the family income.

But if education has given college women access to the professions, it has not given them access to the jobs or status available to educated men. Despite all the publicity about women's changing position in the work force, traditional status and salary differentials remain. A recent study found that among whites the gap in the starting salaries of men and women increased between 1970 and 1980. Even more telling is the persistence of the "wage gap": In 1985 women's wages were about 64 percent of men's, up only 1 percent from 1939. Continued sex segregation of the labor force accounts for the persistence of the problem. [68]

There are signs of change, but not all of them point to greater flexibility. The educational gap is closing, in some respects at least. Women—currently more than half of all undergraduates—still cluster in the arts and humanities; but fewer are majoring in education, and more are taking science and business courses. Women also constitute a large proportion of medical and law students (often as much as one-third). But those in demanding jobs are also marrying later and less often, having fewer children, and having them later in life, a situation that suggests at least a partial return to the demographic conditions that accompanied the achievements of American women in the late nineteenth century. [69] These trends indicate

[68] *New York Times*, January 16, 1984, pp. 1, B-10; Sylvia Ann Hewlett, A *Lesser Life: The Myth of Women's Liberation in America* (New York: Morrow, 1986): 71–72; Waite, "U.S. Women at Work": 26–33.
[69] Heyns and Bird, "Recent Trends": 50–51; "Women Account for Half of College

that our institutions, especially the family, still make very different demands on women and men. Recent well-publicized accounts of women who give up high-powered careers attest to the persistence of the problem. These formulaic stories are virtual replays of journalistic accounts of the 1920s (and later), when "defections" from careers were also highly publicized. We now know that college graduates of the 1920s did not "retreat" to the home and that graduates of the 1940s and 1950s also worked, but at a later stage of the life cycle.[70]

As historians of higher education and the professions continue to debate the nature of women's professional "progress," it is to be hoped that they will become more sensitive to some of the issues raised here. Women's higher education has received considerable attention of late, but we still have little precise knowledge about its larger intellectual and vocational impact. The curriculum, in particular, has received less attention than it deserves. It is sometimes assumed that except for the introduction of distinctly vocational courses, there were few curricular changes connected with women's entry into higher education. Yet there are indications that the women's colleges, which have been most studied, offered innovative courses and programs in science, the social sciences, and music and art, some of which had a distinctly vocational impact. The availability of specific programs may help account for the selection of particular courses of study, but the class and, for some periods, the religious backgrounds of students may be taken into account in the decision to attend college (including which college) as well as in vocational outcome.[71]

Enrollment in U.S., 3 Other Nations," *Chronicle of Higher Education* (September 17, 1986): 1; *Digest of Education Statistics.*

[70] Stricker, *"Cookbooks and Law Books."* See, for example, Alex Taylor III, "Why Women Managers Are Bailing Out," *Fortune* 114 (August 18, 1986): 16–23.

[71] See Barbara Sicherman, review of Helen Lefkowitz Horowitz, *Alma Mater*, in *History of Educational Quarterly* 27 (Spring 1987): 138–42. On the role of the importance of religion, see Joan Jacobs Brumberg, "The Feminization of Teaching: 'Romantic

Assessments of women's professional history must be based on a more adequate understanding of the ways in which shifting life course patterns have affected women's employment. They must also address the matter of how "progress" is being defined: How many individuals worked and for how long? How many made inroads into "male" professions? How far they advanced up the career ladder? Whether they achieved the goals they set for themselves? Whether they had social impact? The answers to these questions will not necessarily all point in the same direction and may differ from period to period, depending on economic transformations as well as changes in consciousness and culture. Finally, as the work of Anne Firor Scott and others on the unpaid activities of women demonstrates, we must be careful not to assume that "gainful employment" is the sole measure of achievement, fulfillment, or social significance.[72]

Sexism' and American Protestant Denominationalism," *History of Education Quarterly*, 23 (Fall 1983): 379–84.
[72] "On Seeing and Not Seeing—A Case of Historical Invisibility," *Journal of American History* 71 (June 1984): 7–21.

GERALDINE JONCICH CLIFFORD

Women's Liberation and

Women's Professions:

Reconsidering the Past,

Present, and Future

During a well-publicized debate in November 1982 between Phyllis Schlafly and Deidre English, editor of the radical magazine *Mother Jones,* English admitted, "I was not raised to believe I'd ever have a position of authority. I was trained to be a teacher and a social worker—classic feminine occupations." English had worked first at one of the nation's early women's studies programs, at the State University of New York College at Old Westbury. One wonders that she had not yet realized that Mother Jones, and virtually every important feminist leader of the nineteenth century and many of the twentieth—from Lucretia Mott, Lucy Stone, Susan B. Anthony, the Grimké sisters, Frances Willard, Jane Swisshelm, Carrie Chapman Catt, and Jeannette Rankin to, in our own times, Shirley Chisholm and Geraldine Ferraro—had *first* exercised

GERALDINE JONCICH CLIFFORD *is professor of education at the University of California at Berkeley.*

authority from the teacher's platform and gained their initial experience as a "public person" *as schoolteachers.*

Considering Mary Lyon's own experience as a teacher, her reasons for founding Mount Holyoke Seminary, and the very high proportion of those graduating from Mount Holyoke who became teachers, it is especially appropriate to consider the status of the so-called traditional women's career fields in the context of feminism. Unlike its predecessor movements, contemporary feminism operates through its various organs—feminist scholarship, women's studies programs, *MS* magazine, consciousness-raising groups, and the like—to devalue and denigrate a range of college women's fields of study and work, leading at least some feminist women to feel guilty, inadequate, and lacking in self-esteem and status. Modern feminism, a movement committed to unfettered choice, thereby limits the choices available to "liberated women" and deprives the social and human services sector of society of the talent and potential feminist leadership that it sorely requires. The women's movement's dismissive and sometimes harsh repudiation of "traditional women's fields" creates a personal crisis for the young woman considering teaching, nursing, social work, librarianship, home economics, housewifery, or an English major, and creates a social crisis, in declaring educational, welfare, and cultural concerns to be "unprogressive," "unfulfilling," and "traditional concessions" to sexual stereotypes.

Before Mount Holyoke chose to identify itself as a women's college, American women had already achieved an unprecedented visibility in formal education. It was an achievement largely of the nineteenth century and one which brought America's women to a place that women do not yet hold in most societies of the world.[1] If we look first at the elite sector—

---

[1] Patricia L. McGrath, *The Unfinished Assignment: Equal Education for Women.* Worldwatch Paper 7 (Washington, D.C.: Worldwatch Institute, 1976).

at high school graduates, college women, and college faculty—women were well represented before 1900. At a time when only about 10 percent of teenagers were attending high school, the majority of high school graduates were women. When about 4 percent of young people were going to college, women constituted 40 percent of the college population. A higher percentage of faculty members in postsecondary education were women in 1870 than in 1970. With regard to mass education—to the eight grades of common schooling which were becoming a universal experience in the nineteenth century—girls of 1900 were at least equal to boys in school attendance. Moreover, women had become the majority of teachers in both primary and secondary schools.[2]

These achievements, particularly women's dominance of secondary teaching, distinguished American culture from others and changed the educational challenge confronting feminist leaders; the struggle had become less one of ensuring access to education for women than of answering the perplexing question, in the words of one feminist, "What are they going to do with their education after they get it?" In an 1859 address, "On Women's Position as Regards Wages," Caroline Dahl—lecturer, feminist, and former teacher—insisted on employment undifferentiated by gender: "I ask for women free, untrammeled access to all fields of labor." Many women were choosing teaching, however, a calling that promised both eco-

[2] Lucille A. Pollard, *Women on College and University Faculties: A Historical Survey and a Study of Their Present Academic Status* (New York: Arno Press, 1977); Susan Carter, "Academic Women Revisited: An Empirical Study of Changing Patterns of Women's Employment as College and University Faculty, 1890–1963," *Journal of Social History* 14 (1981): 675–99; Geraldine Joncich Clifford, Introduction to *Academic Women in America: Women Professors in Coeducational Universities, 1880–1937* (New York: Feminist Press, forthcoming). The growth of the modern corporation and the invention of the typewriter and telephone meant new opportunities for educated women to join the work force in clean and respectable employment. When we examine the work patterns of women high school graduates, we find them concentrated disproportionately in clerical occupations. Clerical work was on its way to becoming the largest employer of women high school graduates.

nomic independence and social respect. In fact, teaching school was beginning to be considered "women's work."[3]

It was widely believed in the early twentieth century that as the barriers to the higher education of women came down, women would enter the liberal occupations and professions. Instead, sex segregation in the workplace either persisted or was reproduced in new occupations. Every United States census from 1900 to 1980 found women workers concentrated in occupations where most of their fellow workers (often 70 or 80 percent of them) were women. The largest categories of female professionals were concentrated in teaching, nursing, librarianship, social work, and home economics. Indeed, half of all women professionals are schoolteachers. Conversely, in the so-called traditionally male professions women were poorly represented at the turn of the century and, despite clear advances, remain underrepresented. Women constituted just 3 percent of attorneys in 1920; they received 30 percent of law degrees conferred in 1980. Women were 6 percent of physicians and 2 percent of dentists in 1910; they took 23 percent of medical and 13 percent of dentistry degrees in 1980. Women remain, however, three-quarters of all those who prepare to teach.[4]

Correspondingly, sex differentiation exists among and within

---

[3] Geraldine Joncich Clifford, "'Marry, Stitch, Die, or Do Worse': Educating Women for Work in America," in *Work, Youth, and Schooling: Historical Perspectives on Vocationalism in American Education*, eds. Harvey Kantor and David B. Tyack, (Stanford, Calif.: Stanford University Press, 1982): 222–68. Caroline Healey Dall, *The College, the Market, and the Court; or Woman's Relation to Education, Labor, and Law* (1867; reprint Boston: Rumford Press, 1914): 135.

[4] National Center for Education Statistics, *Digest of Education Statistics: 1982* (Washington, D.C.: National Center for Education Statistics, 1982): 118, 126, 127; U.S. Department of Commerce, Bureau of the Census, *Statistical Abstract of the United States: 1981*, 101st Edition (Washington, D.C.: Government Printing Office, 1981): 167. In 1972, among those receiving bachelor's degrees in education, women were 74 percent; in 1982 the comparable figure was 76 percent. In Lois Weis, "Progress but No Parity: Women in Higher Education," *Academe* (November–December 1985): 29–33.

the educational institutions that prepare, or fail to prepare, women for the world of work. The late nineteenth and early twentieth centuries created effectively sex-segregated or sex-specific departments. For women this meant specializing in education, child development, home economics, social welfare, or fine arts. Another phenomenon, one that even troubled male college educators in the early twentieth century, was the concentration of women in certain fields within the liberal arts and humanities. Charles Van Hise, the progressive president of the University of Wisconsin, noted in 1907 that women outnumbered men in seven of thirteen state university colleges of liberal arts and sciences. If one examined all thirteen institutions, Van Hise calculated that women constituted nearly 53 percent of the liberal arts students. Accordingly, like President William Rainey Harper of the University of Chicago, Van Hise favored sex segregation within liberal arts courses in order to keep men from fleeing the "feminized" humanities. At the elite, all-male institutions of the Northeast the principal argument for resisting coeducation was that once institutionalized, the "culture courses," as they were called, would become the preserve of women. Thus, red-blooded males might be driven out by "sex repulsion," leaving the liberal arts wan and timid. A more common response to the possibilities of women's enrollment was to assign quotas limiting their numbers or to impose higher entrance requirements for women. The City College of New York, Stanford, Cornell, Michigan, and Pennsylvania State University were among institutions that adopted such practices.[5]

---

[5] Charles R. Van Hise, "Educational Tendencies in State Universities," *Educational Review* 34 (1907): 512; Harold S. Wechsler, "An Academic Gresham's Law: Group Repulsion as a Theme in American Higher Education," *Teachers College Record* 82 (1981): 566–86. At Pennsylvania State University, for example, the ratio of women to male undergraduates was set at 1:2.5. Jonah Churgin, *The New Woman and the Old Academe: Sexism and Higher Education* (Roslyn Heights, N.Y.: Libra Publishers, 1978): 56–57. In addition to sex segregation within educational institutions, one also

In 1889 the British gadfly intellectual Grant Allen responded to an article by American sociologist Lester Frank Ward which had dealt with women and the question of evolution. Ward was mistaken, Allen asserted; women were *not*, in fact, "our better halves." Instead, he contended:

> I believe it to be true that she is very much less the race than man; that she is, indeed, not even half the race at present, but rather the part of it told specially off for the continuance of the species. . . . She is the sex specified to reproductive necessities. All that is distinctively human is man—the field, the ship, the mine, the workshop; all that is truly woman is merely reproductive—the home, the nursery, the schoolroom. There are women, to be sure, who inherit much of male faculty, and some of these prefer to follow male avocations; but in so doing they for the most part unsex themselves; they fail to perform satisfactorily their maternal functions.[6]

It was the uncommon woman, to be sure, who wanted to unsex herself.

Teaching was traditional work in the sense that women had been teaching in the home and in very limited kinds of schools for ages.[7] Women had worked as nuns, creating among the gentlewomen of Europe a class of women frequently more educated than their husbands. These religious women became

finds men and women distributing themselves differently among the types of institutions, universities and technical institutes having a preponderance of men while liberal arts colleges, former state teachers colleges, and two-year colleges are the schools with disproportionate numbers of women.

[6] Grant Allen, "Women's Place in Nature," *Forum* 7 (1889): 258, 263. The phrase *told specially off* means "assigned" in this quotation.

[7] Ruth Bloch points out that the emphasis on and idealization of mother as teacher was less an ancient, honorable, and well-accepted role than it was itself a sign of changing family norms. In the nineteenth century the father's role as guide and teacher was being transferred to the mother of the family. Ruth M. Bloch, "American Feminine Ideals in Transition: The Rise of the Moral Mother," *Feminist Studies* (1978): 100–26.

so influential that the male hierarchy of the church thought it necessary to suppress their orders. Laywomen became governesses, increasingly important work for women with the rise of the middle classes in Europe. Women ran "dame schools," which are frequently dismissed by historians as mere custodial institutions, although recent work concludes that they were extremely important in providing education to various classes. Women also ran "select" and subscription schools in colonial America in numbers substantial enough to have left a historical record.

Teaching is an important subject not only because it attracted the largest part of the graduates of Mount Holyoke and other prestigious women's colleges but for several other reasons. First, historically teaching has been, and remains, a mass experience of women. As feminist historian Carroll Smith-Rosenberg observes, one cannot accept a revisionist women's history that views with suspicion an analysis of the experiences of the average woman.[8] Nor can one hold oneself superior in insight to women of the past or present, dismissing their perceptions of what brings greater autonomy, power, happiness, fulfillment. Second, teaching as women's work and teaching as the chief employment of educated women offer some fascinating historiographic challenges. Feminist historians and social scientists are beginning to break out of the "observational bias" of which Carol Gilligan has written: "Implicitly adopting the male life as the norm, they have tried to fashion women out of masculine cloth."[9] Third, teachers who are women are, and have been, strategically positioned; they are part of the daily socializing experiences of millions of young girls and boys. And fourth, teaching today needs able women recruits and offers them unparalleled opportunities to reshape the occupation.

[8] Ellen DuBois, Carroll Smith-Rosenberg, and others, "Politics and Culture in Women's History: A Symposium," *Feminist Studies* (1980): 26–64.
[9] Carol Gilligan, "Woman's Place in Man's Life Cycle," *Harvard Educational Review* 49 (1979): 432.

The best statistical data we have on the place of teaching in the life histories of women come from a study using census records and various local sources of data for native-born women in Massachusetts during the period from 1830 to 1860. In any given year only 2 percent of women were in teaching, the great majority of women being employed at home, but fully one in four women taught school at some time in her life. Massachusetts was atypical since the feminization of teaching began there, and as late as 1900 the state had the nation's highest ratio of women to men teachers. Nonetheless, what happened in Massachusetts eventually happened, to nearly the same extent, everywhere in the country. The constant turnover in teaching, characteristic of teachers of both sexes, perpetually generated vacancies in schoolrooms. Increasingly after 1830 these vacancies were filled disproportionately by women.[10]

Another way to suggest the importance of the teaching experience in American women's social history is to note that at no time between 1870 and 1980 did teaching fall below fifth place in the list of the ten leading occupations of all adult women workers. Teaching recruited broadly from the working class, the middle class, and the upper middle class. It recruited immigrant women much earlier than many people realized. Lotus Coffman discovered that native-born daughters of foreign-born parents constituted 27 percent of all women teachers in 1910.[11] Teaching recruited very heavily among black women, as racially segregated schools were established by law and custom. By 1920 teachers ranked seventh among the occupations of all black women workers.

Even before college graduation was expected of prospective teachers, we find that the schoolroom attracted the largest proportions of college women who ever sought employment. This was true in both coeducational and women's institutions. In

[10] Richard M. Bernard and Maris A. Vinovskis, "The Female School Teacher in Ante-Bellum Massachusetts," *Journal of Social History* 10 (1977): 332–45.
[11] Lotus D. Coffman, *The Social Composition of the Teaching Population* (New York: Teachers College, Columbia University, 1911): 55.

1896 Kate Holladay Claghorn (who went on to become the first paid employee of the Association of Collegiate Alumnae, the predecessor to the American Association of University Women) declared that nine of ten women college graduates who worked in paid employment went into teaching. In the same year the Massachusetts Bureau of Labor Statistics ranked the occupations of women with college or other special training. Teaching was first, far ahead of other occupations; then came librarianship, stenography, nursing, journalism, and clerical work.[12] A 1912 study of five women colleges found that 54 percent of their graduates were in the teaching profession. The institution with the lowest percentage of graduates teaching was Vassar at 31 percent; Vassar resisted offering even minimal work in pedagogy until 1925.[13] The institution with the highest percentage was, not surprisingly, Mount Holyoke, at 74 percent. Similarly, a 1918 census of 12,000 graduates of nine eastern colleges found that 83.5 percent of women who had ever been employed had been employed as teachers.[14] For the twenty-year period 1889 to 1908, the percentage of women graduates who became teachers grew from 18 to 39 percent. Bryn Mawr College, which stood virtually alone among elite women's colleges in its public commitment to producing career women, graduated higher proportions of teachers than did Wellesley College or the University of Michigan, both of them institutions less devoted to the Bryn Mawr principle that "our failures only marry."[15]

[12] Claghorn and the Massachusetts survey data are cited in Roberta Frankfort, *Collegiate Women: Domesticity and Career in Turn-of-the-Century America* (New York: New York University Press, 1977): 90–91.
[13] An Association of Collegiate Alumnae survey in 1915 found, however, that of 2,363 Vassar graduates responding, nearly 80 percent of those who had ever worked taught at some time; among working alumnae, more than 63 percent had worked only as teachers. Debra Herman, "College and After: The Vassar Experiment in Women's Education, 1861–1924" (Ph.D. diss., Stanford University, 1979): 234, 248.
[14] Mabel Robinson, *The Curriculum of the Woman's College*. Bureau of Education Bulletin, 1918, No. 6 (Washington, D.C.: Government Printing Office, 1918): 120.
[15] Frankfort compares graduates of Wellesley, Bryn Mawr, and the University of

Today there are some 2.5 million public school teachers in the United States. At the elementary school level women constitute some 85 percent of the instructors. In the secondary schools women teachers are just under 50 percent of the faculty, down from about 80 percent at the turn of the century, but since women predominate among those preparing to become teachers, they are expected to increase their share again in the years ahead.

Alice Freeman Palmer was one of the many important women of the nineteenth and early twentieth centuries who had been a teacher; her mother was also a teacher and had supported her husband and children. Palmer argued that teaching and philanthropic work were ideal employments for educated women whose home responsibilities permitted them some leisure time. Women excel, she wrote, in "the characteristic employments of housekeeping, teaching, and ministering to the afflicted."[16] With statistics like those that have been cited, and notions like Palmer's placing teaching securely within "women's sphere," it is not surprising that many scholars of women's history have dismissed or failed to look at teaching's feminist potentialities. But a more careful reading of Palmer finds her advocating, before the graduates of Mount Holyoke Seminary, the creation of woman-run institutions in a vast empire as powerful as Victoria's.[17] Years of research in the personal writings of American women teachers has led me to

Michigan in *Collegiate Women*. After teachers, the group next most numerous among their graduates was college teachers, where the figures ranged from 2 to 20 percent; then clerical work, 1 to 8 percent; social work, 1 to 18 percent; librarians, 1 to 2 percent; doctors and lawyers, 1 to 4 percent; other miscellaneous employments, 4 to 8 percent. Those who never joined the labor force after college ranged from Bryn Mawr's 10 percent to 65 and 66 percent at Wellesley and Michigan.

[16] Alice Freeman Palmer, "Women's Education at the World's Fair," quoted in Frankfort, *Collegiate Women*: 41.

[17] Alice Freeman, in *Semi-Centennial Celebration of Mount Holyoke Seminary, 1837–1887*, ed. Sarah L. Stowe (South Hadley, Mass.: Mount Holyoke Seminary, 1888): 137–38.

conclude that feminist historians have erred in ignoring teaching and other women's professions in thinking about changes leading to changes in consciousness and liberation struggles. To look intensively at teachers as feminists, political activists, officeholders, and community leaders is to become critical of the tendency to dismiss or underestimate such fields because of their legitimation within "women's sphere." Although hers is purportedly a history of women and professions, Barbara J. Harris excludes teaching because like domestic science, the education it required was ostensibly designed "to train women for their proper roles."[18] In her 1974 book *Women in America*, Edith Hoshino Altbach does not have an index entry for teachers. In one of her few references to them she writes that "of the professions, nursing and schoolteaching offered the path of least resistance to women."[19] This conventional historiography has been ill informed and anachronistic. Historians have overlooked important facts and failed to put themselves in the historical positions of their objects of study.

First, today's female-intensive professions (which male sociologists label "semi-professions") were *not* traditionally female fields. Nursing, office and sales work, and librarianship were male careers long before they became "women's work." And women's ways into these fields were strewn with obstacles and recriminations. Second, over the past two or three centuries education gradually moved out of families, out of apprenticeship, and out of Sunday schools and became reestablished in church schools, endowed schools, and particularly tax-supported schools. If women had not been able to pursue teaching careers in the schools, then, rather than having gained some-

---

[18] Geraldine Joncich Clifford, "Teaching as a Seedbed of Feminism," unpublished paper, Fifth Berkshire Conference on Women's History, Vassar College, June 16, 1981; Barbara J. Harris, *Beyond Her Sphere: Women and the Professions in American History* (Westport, Conn.: Greenwood Press, 1978): 59.
[19] Edith Hoshino Altbach, *Women in America* (Lexington, Mass.: D. C. Heath, 1974): 56.

thing not much worth having, they would have lost something quite important to their influence and independence. Teaching, wherever performed, is a powerful molder of human beings; recognizing this, religious and political leaders have always tried to exercise control over those who teach the young. Furthermore, what women schoolteachers gained along with their wages was something larger than their roles as "teachers" within the family circle: influence over the children (and especially over the *sons*) of the entire community. There are additional grounds on which to reconsider the historical relationships of teaching to women's liberation. Admitting women into public and private colleges in the later nineteenth century, so as to upgrade the American teaching profession in general, greatly hastened the triumph of coeducation as the American norm. In the process women students gained access to most of the nation's major institutions.[20]

Let it suffice to emphasize that we not be misled by the domestic analogy and teaching's linkage to the prescriptive "cult of true womanhood." Because women reformers oftentimes exalted motherhood and the sanctity of sisterhood, or because women teachers were called gentle, patient, pious, and non-acquisitive, does not mean we can easily dismiss the expansive potentialities of their work of "domestic feminism." As historian Anne Scott has remarked, women's ability to structure institutions for their own and society's benefit is "one of the best kept secrets in American history. The overt purpose is education or philanthropy or reform, or building an art museum, or starting something like the juvenile protection agency or the Freedman's Bureau, and so on. . . . But there's

[20] Deborah Fitts, "Una and the Lion: The Feminization of District Schoolteaching and Its Effects on the Role of Students and Teachers in Nineteenth-Century Massachusetts," in *Regulated Children / Liberated Children: Education in Psychohistorical Perspective*, ed. Barbara Finklestein (New York: Psychohistory Press, 1979); Geraldine Joncich Clifford, "'Shaking Dangerous Questions from the Crease': Gender and American Higher Education," *Feminist Issues* 3 (Fall 1983): 3–62.

also the covert purpose, which is to form an acceptable framework in which women can have a public life."[21] We must remember that women and their male supporters were effectively arguing for an expanded role for women before audiences of conservative men and women who would otherwise have been alarmed and made more resistant. Instead of looking at the prescriptive literature, let us think about how the opportunity, the experience, the financial and psychic independence that teaching offered, affected women's lives and consciousness.

If one looks at notable women, one can certainly find women whose own lives gave the lie to the notion of teaching as a restricted sphere. As founder and head of Mount Holyoke Mary Lyon was enabled to lead a life that was as close as any woman conceivably could get to the quintessential male career of that time, that of a clergyman-teacher. If one looks at the masses of women "of the middling sort," by examining diaries and family correspondence, one sees in teaching the opportunity to lead a public life at a time when a public life was thought inappropriate to women. To organize a school, deal with the community's leaders, put on ceremonies, and travel about collecting the wages owed from cash-poor patrons was to take on major responsibility in a time when the public world was not yet considered the appropriate place for women. As teachers women exercised control over nonfamily men and provided for themselves in the process, gaining self-confidence and higher expectations of what they were owed in economic and professional terms. There were many, like the nineteenth-century radical feminist Lucy Stone, who did better by persuasion what her male predecessor had failed to do by force, he having been

---

[21] Anne Firor Scott and William H. Chafe, "What We Wish We Knew About Women: A Dialogue," in *Clio Was a Woman: Studies in the History of American Women*, ed. Mabel E. Deutrich and Virginia C. Purdy (Washington, D.C.: Howard University Press, 1980): 10. See also Anne Firor Scott, "What, Then, Is the American: This New Woman?," *Journal of American History* 65 (1978): 679–703.

tossed out in the snow by his pupils. As teachers women forged bonds with other women, with women students, with mothers of their students, and with the women with whom they boarded. Florence Howe is almost alone among feminist scholars and activists in warning that in our desire to integrate women in nontraditional areas, we must not forget the traditional female professions, especially teaching. She asserts that the struggles women waged to enter teaching, nursing, and librarianship are not yet won and that the gains made should be consolidated: "To focus feminist energies on them now would be to develop 'womanpower' to change three of the most important service institutions in the society." In *Women and the Power to Change*, Howe argues that feminists must recognize the crucial role that teachers play in the sex role socialization of young people:

Why encourage the most talented women to enter a physics laboratory rather than a school superintendent's office or a department of educational administration? Why is it more important to spread a thin tokendom of women through the nontraditional kingdoms rather than to attempt a transformation of the traditional ghettos themselves—especially if one of those, the public school system, is responsible for the perpetuation of sex stereotyping and the low aspirations of women?[22]

Now is the time to recognize the contribution women have made to education. It is time to assist women's push into other careers in education—into responsible positions within teaching and into school administration and policy positions in education. In light of the movement of the 1980s finally to professionalize teaching, there are unprecedented opportuni-

[22] Florence Howe, ed., *Women and the Power to Change* (New York: McGraw-Hill, 1975): 166; Introduction ("The Teacher and the Women's Movement") to Nancy Frazier and Myra Sadker, *Sexism in School and Society* (New York: Harper & Row, 1973): xi–xv.

ties for women both to take back the school principalships that they once held, then lost and to insert themselves into other key positions in the public school system, from school district offices to state government. To do so will enhance the emergence of a kind of educational leadership that will empower teachers, both women and men.

It was a bright, insightful woman, a Boston area teacher, who said in 1981, "I really feel that a strong basis for the backlash against teachers is that [this is a field in which] now women are earning equal to men. How dare they?!"[23] In 1966 some 22 percent of all entering college freshmen wanted to become teachers; by 1982 less than 5 percent planned teaching careers. The decline in quantity, in part a result of "teacher bashing," has been accompanied by a probable but less easily established drop in the quality of prospective teachers.[24] In this century, and probably in much of the nineteenth as well, we are reasonably sure that teaching has recruited brighter, more academically able women and women of higher status than male teachers. Historical studies of the occupational and educational backgrounds of teachers report that the women have come from families of higher economic and social status than their male counterparts. The reasons for the difference lie in large part in differential opportunities for the two sexes. Today this situation may have changed. There is evidence that those planning to teach are not, on average, the most intelligent of college students. Moreover, retention in teaching is negatively correlated with academic record and scholastic aptitude. A

[23] The sense among teachers that their work has been demoted from "calling" to a "job" is also reported in Sarah Freedman, Jane Jackson, and Katherine Boles, *The Effects of Institutional Structures on Teachers*, Final Report, National Institute of Education Grant No. G-81-0031 (Lexington, Mass.: Boston Women's Teachers' Group, 1982): 75.

[24] On the basis of analyzing a large sample of 1980 high school seniors, Timothy Z. Keith and Ellis Page conclude that "the reported tendency for teaching to attract those of lesser ability may be an effect, *now*, primarily of females [and blacks]"; "Now Who Aspires to Teach?," *Educational Researcher* 12 (June 1983): 13.

number of studies have concluded that the academic and, if you will, intellectual potentialities in the corps of teachers are lower in the eighties than they were in the sixties and possibly appreciably lower than they were, for example, in the job-scarce thirties.[25]

Patti Laffer argues that feminism has exacerbated the failure of education to recruit more career-conscious and feminist women.[26] The feminist assault on male professional hege-mony has resulted in many women's choosing "male-inten-sive" careers. The women graduates of leading colleges are going into other fields. In 1982 an issue of Mount Holyoke's alumnae magazine proudly reported that for the first time, M.B.A. aspirants would exceed the numbers intending to teach. Reporting on her travels about the country, Florence Howe noted that she met "intrepid feminist teachers" leaving public education for law school or Ph.D. programs in other fields.[27] If we care about education, we must have teachers better than the ones we are now attracting. This does not mean that intel-ligence, good education, and academic aptitude are the only requirements for effective teaching, but they are essentials.

It is encouraging that law, business, medicine, and engi-neering are getting far larger numbers of bright women than they once had, but to raise the occupational aspirations of women graduates while simultaneously lowering the intellec-

[25]For example, see National Education Association (NEA), *Status of the American Public School Teachers*, 1970–71; "The Status of the American Public School Teacher," *Research Bulletin of the NEA* 35 (February 1957): 9; William Wattenberg et al., "Social Origins of Teachers—A Northern Industrial City," in *The Teacher's Role in American Society*, ed. Lindley Stiles (New York: Harper, 1957): 13–22; Geraldine Joncich Clifford, "Daughters into Teachers: Educational and Demographic Influences on the Transformation of Teaching into 'Women's Work,'" *History of Education Review* 12 (1983): 15–28; Phillip C. Schlechty and Victor S. Vance, "Recruitment, Selection, and Retention: The Shape of the Teaching Force," *Elementary School Journal* 83 (1983): 469–87.

[26]Patti Laffer, "Reclaiming Our Profession: Towards a Feminist Theory of Public Education," unpublished paper, April 1981.

[27]Howe, *Women and the Power to Change*: 167.

tual level of teachers is a poor bargain, damaging to the long-term interests of the women's movement. It is appropriate that women are venturing and feeling free to venture more widely in the working world. Free choice should be the right of capable, ambitious women, as it has been the right of men. But it should be a truly free choice. Is it possible that in their zeal feminists have actually reduced choice by suggesting that being *merely* a teacher, *merely* a nurse, *merely* a librarian or a social worker is analogous to being *"merely* a housewife" and hence, if not deplorable, at least regrettable?

Gene Agre and Barbara Finkelstein have employed the terms *domestic feminists* and *economic feminists* to analyze the current women's movement in its posture toward educational policy and practice. Economic feminists, reformers who put women's economic independence and economic power at the forefront, were the first and most vocal representatives of the contemporary organized women's movement.

Accepting at some level the justice of a system of economic rewards and punishments that devalues, if it does not punish, the roles of those who are responsible for the daily delivery of personal services—mothers, teachers, nurses, secretaries, waitresses, wives—economic feminists have attempted to enlist the schools in an effort to disentangle women from the supportive role, seeking instead to teach them how to compete, to enjoy winning, how to become less vulnerable to the subtleties of human interaction. . . . Proceeding on the assumption that women's work is inevitably less valuable than that of men, they have emphasized the need to counsel girls out of traditional female professions. . . . [I]n the process, economic feminists have been contributing, however subtly or inadvertently, to the denigration of women's traditional function, as well as their traditional status.[28]

[28]Gene P. Agre and Barbara Finkelstein, "Feminism and School Reform: The Last Fifteen Years," *Teachers College Record* 80 (1978): 307–15.

Henry Adams once wrote that the woman who is known only through a man is known wrong. If men devalue nurturing, teaching, and other human service occupations, or unpaid labor in civic or philanthropic activities, should feminists do so as well? If men shun work with children, the dependent, the helpless, should feminists also adopt that perspective? Why should feminists—as scholars, as counselors of young women—perpetuate the profound sexism that makes men's occupations more important and more valuable; that gives men preference over women in virtually all employments, including those in which women are the majority of the practitioners; that leads many women to conclude that they can raise the prestige, quality, and effectiveness of their professions only by recruiting more men and, if need be, by paying them more; and that says that the congruence of work to family life is somehow unworthy and evidence of a "lack of commitment"? It would be tragically ironic if the "enemy within" flourished while the "enemy without" was being vanquished.

ANN FERGUSON

Woman's Moral Voice:

Superior, Inferior,

or Just Different?

James ("Jim") Corbett, a fifty-year-old Quaker, retired rancher
and Harvard-educated philosopher, is a member of the sanctuary movement. His reason for illegally smuggling political
refugees from El Salvador and Guatemala into the United States
is quoted by the *Boston Globe* (January 27, 1985) as follows:
"The most elementary act of doing justice is entering into a
protective relationship with the persecuted. This is prophecy.
This is the Bible. . . ." A woman identified only as Wendy by
the *Globe* gives two reasons for becoming involved in the sanctuary movement—her religion and being a mother: "If I live
my faith, I have to help people in need. . . . Secondly, if my
children ever fled for their lives, I would hope another mother
would take them in. I am a real mother at heart. How can you

ANN FERGUSON *is professor of philosophy and women's studies at the
University of Massachusetts at Amherst.*

turn someone down when they're in such trouble?"

Seyla Benhabib, a philosopher at Boston University, uses these quotations to contrast what cognitive and educational psychologist Carol Gilligan calls two moral voices: an ethics of justice and rights, characteristic of men's moral thinking, and one of care and responsibility characteristic of women. As Benhabib explains, Jim Corbett's way of reasoning for his sanctuary involvement appeals to a hierarchy of moral rules. The moral obligation to respect any other human being has a higher claim on a person (the claim of justice and rights) than the moral obligation to respect the legal code of the United States. Wendy's argument, on the other hand, appeals to the value of helping people in need. She imagines the people as falling under her protection as a live mother rather than an abstract defender of justice.[1]

Gilligan's work stems directly from the insights of the neo-Freudian feminist analysis of gender differences of Nancy Chodorow. Such new interdisciplinary feminist theory has posed exciting challenges to the male-dominated disciplines of philosophy and cognitive psychology. It also has important implications for women in higher education more generally. I will contrast the situation of feminists in higher education today with that of their foremothers and sisters in the first-wave women's movement of the nineteenth century. I will argue that we are faced with a paradox similar to that experienced by early agitators for women's rights to education. The paradox is this: Though the vast majority of Americans now believe that women ought to have equal rights with men, the cultural norms still maintain a sexual division of labor at home and in the work force which perpetuates sexist gender distinctions and differences.

The paradox raises two questions of concern to feminist

[1] Seyla Benhabib, "The Generalized and the Concrete Other: Visions of the Autonomous Self," in *Proceedings of the Conference on Women and Morality*, State University of New York at Stony Brook, March 22–24, 1985.

educators of women. First, should feminists hold that these gender differences, genetically or socially imposed, create women with values and a moral voice superior to men, inferior to men, or merely different? For were one to assume that women's moral voice is socially constructed as inferior to men's, women's education should then attempt to reconstruct this voice, to raise it to men's level. On the other hand, were women's moral voice to be considered superior to men's, then not only should women's education insist upon cultivating this voice, but feminists should also seek ways to assist men in acquiring this perspective. Second, aside from evaluating the differences between men's and women's values, how should women's education prepare women to deal with these differences as they prepare for careers? Should feminists encourage women to choose careers primarily peopled by women so as to reduce the cognitive dissonance that might otherwise occur? Or should feminists devise coping mechanisms that will aid women students to fit comfortably into professions that are primarily male?[2]

These two questions are not unique to our generation. Indeed, they have been present from the beginning of women's higher education in the United States. Before we engage present thinking on these topics, it will be instructive to sketch nineteenth-century feminist views on these questions. Nineteenth-century feminists who advocated higher education for women were faced with a version of the same ideological paradox feminists face today. On the one hand, feminists such as Catharine Beecher advocated higher education for women in order to increase their ability to do their own work ably in their "separate sphere" of the home, where it was presumed woman's moral voice should be exercised.[3] Thus, though Beecher was the head of a seminary for girls, her philosophy was indistinguishable from that of the founding fathers of the first coed-

[2] I'd like to acknowledge the valuable editorial assistance of Joan Cocks, whose help vastly improved the final version of this paper.
[3] Eleanor Flexner, *Century of Struggle* (New York: Atheneum, 1972).

ucational and interracial college, Oberlin College. In its stated objectives, higher education was to improve women's status by bringing about the "elevation of the female character, bringing within the reach of the misjudged and neglected sex all the instructive privileges which hitherto have unreasonably distinguished the leading sex from theirs."[4]

Such education for women was not to be a means to erase the separate spheres and "callings" of the sexes. Rather, "Oberlin's attitude was that women's high calling was to be the mothers of the race and that they should stay within that special sphere in order that future generations should not suffer for the want of devoted and undistracted mothercare. If women became lawyers, ministers, physicians, lecturers, politicians or any sort of 'public character' the home would suffer from neglect."[5]

On the other hand, Mary Lyon, the founder of Mount Holyoke Seminary, held an integrationist position. Founded in 1837, Mount Holyoke was the first institution of higher education for women to offer a course of study similar to those at the men's colleges of the day. Lyon firmly believed that all women, rich or poor, should have the opportunity for a higher education. This was not merely to design them to be better wives and mothers. Rather, women must have the possibility of working as professionals and participating in public life. Women's minds, she thought, were constituted the same as their masculine counterparts. Thus, given opportunity, discipline, and direction, they could master the same subject matter as men. These ideas were quite revolutionary for her day, though now, of course, they are commonplace liberal ideas.[6]

In the nineteenth century higher education for women had

---

[4] Quoted in Robert S. Fletcher, *History of Oberlin College to the Civil War* (Oberlin, Ohio: Oberlin College, 1943): 1:373; also quoted in Flexner, *Century of Struggle*: 30.
[5] Fletcher, *History of Oberlin College*: 291, quoted in Flexner, *Century of Struggle*: 30.
[6] Flexner, *Century of Struggle*: 31–36.

radical consequences no matter whether the founders of the college held a "separate spheres" or an integrationist perspective. It is ironic that Lucy Stone, one of the finest antislavery and feminist orators of her day, and Antoinette Brown Blackwell, the first woman to be ordained a minister, were some of the first women to graduate from the "separate spheres" college of Oberlin. Clearly there was a social contradiction between the "separate spheres" ideology and the reality of a higher education that provided women access to information comparable with men's and that enabled women to participate in public life. Lucy Stone felt this contradiction very early, when as the head of her graduating class at Oberlin she refused to write a commencement speech, since social conventions of the day would have required that it be read by a man![7]

Paradoxes analogous to those facing women in the nineteenth century plague women in higher education today. On the one hand, there is the prevalent liberal integrationist ideology that men and women should have equal opportunity to higher education on the basis of their individual merit. On the other hand, sexism continues to exist in personal and structural ways in women's lives. Today this occurs in a fashion more mystifying, particularly for young women, than in the nineteenth century.

Today, though men and women are presumed equal, mothering and housework are still supposed to be "women's work" and are still unremunerated by either men in the family or the culture as a whole. Thus, separate and unequal spheres for women and men in family life are perpetuated. This unequal division of labor creates a "second shift" of work for professional women who are married and mothers. This was not a problem in the nineteenth century, for professional women expected to remain single or to retire from teaching or other professional work when they married. Today the increasing

---

[7] Ibid., footnote 13 to Ch. 2.

prevalence of divorce puts mothers at risk of being single parents, at which point they also become subject to the double-day problem with a vengeance. Those who come out as lesbians, thus equalizing their emotional and material relations with their love partners, find themselves harassed and ostracized in most conventional social contexts, in ways that close friendships between women were not stigmatized in the nineteenth century.

How does one explain that despite the prevalence of the liberal ideology of gender equality, a strong sexual division of labor still oppresses women? Compared with men's, job opportunities for women are generally less unionized, are less secure, and pay less. How does one explain the unfairness of the double workday for working mothers with children?

Are these differences and inequalities due to the persistence of old social structures set up by traditional inequalities between the sexes? If so, what accounts for the fact that when women are given *choices*— to choose a major in college or a career— they tend to replicate the existing sexual division of labor? Women faculty and graduate students continued to be heavily concentrated in those fields associated with women's traditional sphere of domestic skills: in education, literature, art, nursing, and fields involving communication skills, such as psychological counseling and foreign languages. Do these choices, as well as the lack of full integration of women into male-dominated professions—as physicians, physicists, social scientists, lawyers, business managers, and economists—indicate that women by and large prefer to develop skills that mirror mothering?

Liberal feminists today answer such questions by pointing to the persistence of traditional patriarchal social structures and patterns of women's socialization.[8] These feminists believe that

[8] Betty Friedan, *The Feminine Mystique* (New York: Norton, 1963); Simone de Beauvoir, *The Second Sex* (New York: Knopf, 1963).

such gender differences will die away, as women, potentially rational self-interested agents like men, gain education and greater economic independence, overcome socialized passivity, and learn to control their feelings in male-dominated professional arenas where competitive activity is the norm.

Another strand of contemporary feminist theory approaches the persistence of gender difference somewhat differently. Radical feminist thinkers are strongly critical of the values informing economic and public life and the traditional education which prepares students for that life. The most radical of such thinkers—for example, the philosopher Mary Daly— claim that male values represented in the dominant culture stem from envy over women's procreative and spiritual life-affirming creativity.[9]

The Women's Pentagon Action and the Women's Seneca Peace Camp of the early 1980s linked the threat of nuclear war to militarism, which in turn was thought to be an end product of masculinism. Philosopher Sarah Ruddick argues that the specific tasks of mothering for which all women are socialized, whether or not they become mothers, communicate the values of preservation, growth, and social acceptability for another human life beyond one's own.[10] These values are at odds, ultimately, with war and violence.[11] Ruddick therefore holds out the hope that men who engage in the social task of mothering could develop these values. As of now, however, it seems to follow that men as a group, lacking such a specific practice, have not been socialized to develop these values.

[9] Mary Daly, Gyn/Ecology: The Meta-ethics of Radical Feminism (Boston: Beacon, 1978).
[10] Sarah Ruddick, "Maternal Thinking," Feminist Studies 6 (1980), reprinted in Mothering: Essays in Feminist Theory, ed. Joyce Trebilcot (Totowa, N.J.: Rowman & Allanheld, 1984): 213–30.
[11] Sarah Ruddick, "Preservative Love and Military Destruction: Some Reflections on Mothering and Peace," ibid.: 231–62.

Philosophers Nancy Hartsock and Sandra Harding argue that the sexual division of labor has created a distinctive woman's (and potentially feminist) standpoint which offers a better way of understanding the social order than that of men, who as dominant members of society tend to engage in more abstract, less emotionally rooted tasks, and whose vision is systematically distorted by their positions of power.[12]

Whether or not it holds masculine values absolutely responsible for war and violence, feminist theory on gender difference contends that masculinist *bias*, in both the style and the content of what is taught in college, must be challenged before higher education can achieve the full integration of women into public life. It is not enough to espouse affirmative action programs to redress the inequality of female role models in male-dominated fields, though of course, feminist activists must continue to resist the demolition of affirmative action programs by conservative forces. Even where such affirmative action programs have been successful, however, they have not necessarily challenged the masculinist presuppositions of the field's content and pedagogy. Instead, young women scholars are forced to submerge what gender difference feminist theory argues is their distinctive "feminine voice" and become male-identified. For women, this means assimilation into masculine styles of thinking and pedagogy. It is thus not surprising that many young women, who choose to be professionals yet also aspire to be wives and mothers, gravitate to female-dominated professions, which minimize the juggling of incompatible competitive and nurturant modes of being and thinking.

[12] Nancy Hartsock, *Money, Sex and Power* (New York: Longman, 1983); Sandra Harding, "The Instability of the Analytical Categories of Feminist Theory," *Journal of Women in Culture and Society* 11 (1986): 645–64. Sandra Harding and Merrill Hintikka, eds., *Discovering Reality: Feminist Perspectives on Epistemology, Metaphysics, Methodology and Philosophy of Science* (Dordrecht, Holland: Reidel, 1983). Harding now argues that the feminist epistemological standpoint is an existential project rather than an objective position. See Sandra Harding, *The Science Question in Feminism* (Ithaca, N.Y.: Cornell University Press, 1986).

Gender-difference feminist theory challenges the male bias in philosophical and scientific presuppositions by an approach ironically similar to the ideology underlying the idea of "separate spheres" in the nineteenth century—with one key difference. Nineteenth-century thinkers assumed these differences were innate, designed by a providential nature to assure that the sexes, thus dependent on each other, would continue to reproduce the human race. Most twentieth-century gender-difference theorists, on the contrary, assume that these gender differences are socially constructed. Unlike liberal feminists, who view these socialized differences as *weaknesses* which women need to overcome, gender-difference feminist theorists assume these differences are important *strengths* necessary as a corrective to masculine traits.

One very influential theorist in this camp is the neo-Freudian theorist Nancy Chodorow. She argues that gender differences are socially constructed by mothers' asymmetrical parenting.[13] Girls, having in their mothers gender role models immediately *present* by which to define themselves, develop a concept of self that is the *same* as their significant other and thus develop a permeable ego that defines itself in relation to others. Girls have a secure gender identity but have difficulty achieving a sense of themselves as autonomous individuals.

According to Chodorow, boys have a much more problematic gender identity since male role models are relatively less present for the very young boy. They thus tend to define themselves (and masculinity) as what is *not* feminine, as not the mother. Men find it easier to think of themselves as autonomous from others and thus to compete with each other in groups of peers. Their masculine gender identity is not a personal but positional one (defined by general rules), which

[13] Nancy Chodorow, *The Reproduction of Mothering* (Berkeley, Calif.: Stanford University Press, 1978); cf. also Jane Flax, "The Conflict Between Nurturance and Autonomy in Mother-Daughter Relationships and Within Feminism," *Feminist Studies* 4 (1978): 171–91.

facilitates their participation in social practices that require hierarchical relations to others and abstract rules of the game. Men have a harder time, however, in seeing the *connections* between themselves and others.

Feminist philosophers have generalized these conclusions about personality differences between men and women to argue that Western scientific, political, and philosophical thought, almost entirely developed by men, bears the imprint of the biases of masculine personality in its philosophical assumptions. Thus, Evelyn Fox Keller, Sandra Harding, and Nancy Hartsock have argued that in Western thought the very concept of "science" itself involves the idea of a dualist opposition between humans and nature, in which the latter, like a woman, must be subjugated.[14]

One of the most influential applications of Chodorow's paradigm of gender differences is to be found in Carol Gilligan's work.[15] Like every initial challenge to paradigms in the history of science, however, as it stands, her theory is problematic and requires a dialectical reading to correct and develop it further.

Gilligan uses Chodorow's theory of the differential ego development of masculine and feminine personalities to mount a critique against Lawrence Kohlberg's theory of moral development.[16] Kohlberg, like Jean Piaget, identifies three stages of cognitive development along the path toward mental maturity: first, an egocentric understanding of fairness based on individual need; second, a conception of fairness anchored in the shared conventions of social agreement (i.e., accepting conventional morality to please others); and finally, a principled understanding of fairness resting on a universalized logic of

[14] Keller, "Gender and Science," in Harding and Hintikka, *Discovering Reality:* 187–206.
[15] Carol Gilligan, *In a Different Voice* (Cambridge, Mass.: Harvard University Press, 1982).
[16] Lawrence Kohlberg, *The Philosophy of Moral Development* (San Francisco: Harper & Row, 1981).

equality and reciprocity (i.e., postconventional morality). Kohlberg's criterion for the highest stages of moral reasoning is principled reasoning, that which responds to a moral dilemma by explicating moral principles and then ordering them to defend one's answer of how to handle a conflict of duties. And it turns out that males score much higher at younger ages than females on this scale of moral maturity.[17]

Gilligan argues that Kohlberg's assumptions are responsible for this difference. Kohlberg's scale needs to be bifurcated into two scales, one which charts the path of the "masculine moral voice" and one the "feminine moral voice." The logic characteristic of men involves thinking in terms of abstract rights, while the logic characteristic of women involves an ethic of responsibility which emphasizes the contextual needs and responsibilities of self in relation to others. Since Kohlberg's scale favors argument by principle, it cannot identify women's postconventional thinking, which balances responsibilities to self and others by contextual thinking.

A central problem with Gilligan's "solution" to the problem of gender difference in moral reasoning is her implicit assumption that there is a single generalizable "feminine voice" in moral reasoning which, if not clearly superior to the masculine voice, is not only complementary but an essential supplement for a fully mature, "human" morality. But in fact, this is an unwarranted generalization. A number of women tested scored just as high as, and in some cases higher than, some men on the Kohlberg "Rights/Justice" scale of moral maturity. Interestingly, follow-up studies show that a significant proportion of black women scored higher than white women on the "Rights/Justice" scale. The original sample of Gilligan's study consisted of white middle- and upper-class college students at

[17]The scale also classifies members of highly industrialized Western societies as more mature than members of traditional non-Western societies. Furthermore, Kohlberg can't explain why many of those who score high in moral maturity in college appear to "regress" or slip down several stages in their moral level when retested in later life.

Harvard; hence, even the gender *generalizations* she has made may characterize only white middle-class moral reasoning in advanced industrial societies. Thus, Gilligan's is an inadequate theory of the self and gender. Along with Chodorow, she assumes that men and women have unified egos with differential gender personalities set from childhood.

Instead, we should take a more dialectical perspective. This approach would allow for the possibility that such gender differences in morality (perhaps most often present in white middle-class populations) are characteristic of only one aspect of a complicated human psyche that is often at odds with itself and that therefore cannot be thought, comfortingly, to have only one "essence." If we think of the self as having many parts, some of which are in conflict, we can make better sense out of the apparent dichotomy of masculine and feminine voices. Aspects of our selves are developed by participating in ongoing social practices which insist on certain sets of skills and values. Where different social practices encourage different sets of skills and values that are in conflict, people will develop conflicting aspects of self. This is today true of women in our society who are involved in helping professions, like higher education, nursing, or social work, which call for conflicting skills and values. Those in the helping professions must develop their ability to empathize with others—students, patients, or clients— in order to be successful. But since most women work in large bureaucratic settings where impersonal rules of the game apply, they must also develop a Rights/Justice orientation in self-defense. These women must develop two moral voices, those Gilligan labels "masculine" and "feminine," moral voices that are in unhappy and unharmonious juxtaposition in a single consciousness.

Such a contradiction in ways of thinking and valuing is true not only for women in higher education and the helping professions, but also for those who, because of their "private" family lives, must develop skills at odds with their male colleagues in male-dominated fields. Such a dilemma includes some men who, in sharing housework and child care in the home with their mates, find themselves at odds with their male colleagues at work. It also includes black and other minority women, no matter whether employed as professionals or as wage laborers or not employed at all, who develop a Rights/ Justice orientation in defense against the discrimination of dominant whites, toward whom they cannot afford to take a simple caring orientation.[18]

The presence of both "masculine" and "feminine" identi- fied capacities demonstrates the falsity not only of the thesis that gender differences are a biological given but also the idea that "feminine" and "masculine" voices are socially con- structed within women and men by the early-childhood expe- rience of asymmetrical parenting. The noticeable social differences between men and women that continue to show up in studies, I believe, are caused by the contradictory aspects of social life. For increasing segments of the population, these contradictions are inevitable, especially for black women, who must strengthen their oppositional aspect to survive racism, for career women in large bureaucratic structures, and for women engaged in union struggles in wage labor.

Liberal feminist theorists voice a partial truth by emphasiz- ing that women in male-identified work can pursue their own rational self-interests in competition with other individuals. Neo-Freudian feminist theorists emphasize that socially con- structed gender differences "cause" developmental psychology and moral philosophy to ignore the strengths of the feminine

[18] I do not wish to imply by the emphasis on the social construction of the self that there is no such thing as individuality. Clearly individuals do have a sense of self and values independent of their ongoing relations with others. My point is that individu- ality is a self-conscious construction which tries to make sense out of the often con- flicting practices in which one is engaged. It is one's distinctive relation to the unique set of social interactions that make up one's life (family of origin experience, present family/kin or household living arrangements, conflicting aspects of work life, etc.) which constitutes individuality.

permeable gender personality. The dialectical feminist theory, I propose, however, rejects the idea of a total, unchanging, essential core to masculine and feminine gender personality. Rather, I see people engaged in a process of self-reflection about conflicting aspects of their lives—both oppositional and incorporative—aspects that are exacerbated by changes in the modern organization of wage work and the family.

We are now in a position to offer an answer to the two questions posed at the outset of this paper. Most women (and many men) have both masculine and feminine aspects of self, conflicting moral voices developed through different social practices. These aspects cannot be judged as inferior or superior out of context. But feminist educators who value the strengths of women's incorporational impulses must educate women students in ways to value this aspect of self as an important social resource, whether their careers be in work primarily with men or primarily with women. In order to achieve the American ideal of democratic individualism, women do need to become more like men in the sense of developing a strong oppositional voice—that is, a sense of self as having rights against others and a sense of abstract justice. But to keep such an ideal from being excessively masculinist, women must also defend a woman-centered, feminist ideal of cooperative and caring interaction with others.

With this dialectical ideal in mind, women students can be encouraged to go into either predominantly male or predominantly female professions, with an eye to finding ways of undermining the excessively hierarchical and competitive structure of the former and of supplementing the latter through organizing. Women choosing male professions should understand the importance of building supportive rather than competitive networks with women peers in order to resist male identification and isolation. And they may also consider challenging their male colleagues with visions of less hierarchical, more process-oriented, smaller, and more localized decision-making structures. Such structures may help approximate aspects of the cooperative, caring relations with others that women's traditional work in the home and in some women's professions encourages.[19]

Women who choose primarily women's professions, on the other hand, should learn to organize collectively to demand that their comparable worth as professionals be taken seriously. And in both sorts of profession feminists should influence trade unions and employers to challenge the public/private split of wage and domestic work that burdens mothers with the "second shift" problem by struggling for child care, flexible schedules, and maternity and paternity leave. The combination of a dialectical theory of gender identity with a personal and social ideal that combines democratic individualism and feminist cooperative caring can be the most effective approach of feminist educators in preparing college-educated women for the complex world of work and personal relationships that they will face upon graduation.

[19] My personal view is that such a transformation of American work life is not possible without a simultaneous movement toward a feminist, worker-controlled democratic socialism. But to defend this point would take more time than available in this short paper. For more on this point, see Ann Ferguson, *Blood and the Root: Motherhood, Sexuality and Male Dominance* (New York and London: Routledge, forthcoming).

RUTH SCHMIDT
The Role of Women's Colleges in the Future

During my three years as president of a women's college and the four years prior to that as provost of another in New England, I frequently have been asked by other educators, media persons, and even a sprinkling of our own alumnae whether women's colleges are not now anachronistic, no longer needed. Women's access to almost all educational institutions is now a fact; only a handful of colleges still deny admission to women.

Those of us who form the membership of the Women's College Coalition are very well aware of the fact that the number of women's colleges dropped from 142 in 1972 to 108 in 1985 and that only 2 percent of women undergraduates study in the women's college environment. There are many women's colleges that could boast of enrollment gains in the 1970s and have been bolstered in their commitment by insights from

RUTH SCHMIDT *is president of Agnes Scott College in Decatur, Georgia.*

the women's movement. But even those persons committed to women's education in women's colleges worry about being able to convince enough women students not only of the viability of women's colleges but of the fact that women's colleges are still the *very best* place for women to be educated. Parents, and again, sometimes even our own alumnae, who may recognize that an Agnes Scott College or a Mount Holyoke was the perfect place for them in their time, now believe that the world has changed so drastically that their daughters do not need that special environment for them to develop their full potentials.

Although I did not have the privilege of a women's college education, I am a firm believer in women's colleges. I have heard many personal testimonies to what women's colleges have meant to women in the past and have read research supporting the opportunities which they provide currently. Most important, because I am convinced that there will not be full equality for women in our society in my lifetime, I believe that the need for women's colleges will continue into the future.

I will gladly confess at the outset that I find it impossible to predict, or even to guess, what women's colleges will be like in another 150 years. Therefore, we in higher education have stopped talking about *long-range* planning and have begun to think in terms of *strategic* planning. What are the strategic moves which we can take in the light of our assessment of current realities which will most enhance the women's educational institutions to which we devote our lives? What we have to go on, in thinking about the future, involves, first, those principles which have guided us throughout the history of women's colleges. One might call them the "verities." Secondly, we have the trends of the last ten or fifteen years. These may help us see what is ahead of us in the immediate future.

The verities include our belief that women are worthy. And because society is not convinced of women's total worthiness, we must create and maintain special institutions for women.

This was one of the guiding principles which motivated the creation of women's colleges in an era when women were not invited to attend colleges designed only for men. Not many of these all-male colleges are left anymore; there are only a few liberal arts institutions, such as Wabash, Hampden-Sydney, Morehouse, as well as a few military colleges. These colleges are holdovers from the past. The president of Wabash College, Lewis Salter, when speaking on issues of single sex and coeducation, often calls himself a "dinosaur." But those of us in women's education are well aware that although women are eagerly sought as students in almost all colleges and universities, and although women make up more than half of college and university populations, this has not guaranteed equality of treatment or equality of access to all fields. For example, women's colleges have a history of producing graduates in the sciences (and other disciplines where women are normally underrepresented) which far surpasses the proportion of women who study these subjects in coeducational environments.

Another "verity" of women's colleges is their proportion of women faculty and professional staff: approximately double the average of coeducational colleges and universities. The importance of this fact cannot be overestimated; as Mirra Komarovsky has pointed out, "highest levels of faculty contacts . . . were reported by women in single-sex schools. This advantage held across all majors and at all grade-point average levels. Since the proportion of women faculty is highest in women's colleges, students in such institutions enjoy a considerable advantage, as our findings suggest, in contacts with faculty that provide models to emulate and encouragement through personal interest in student development."[1]

Women's colleges were founded on a belief in women's abilities. And accordingly, women's college graduates have

[1] Mirra Komarovsky, *Women in College: Shaping New Feminine Identities* (New York: Basic Books, 1985): 307.

compiled an enviable record, which continues even in this contemporary age, when there is very little understanding of single sex education. M. Elizabeth Tidball's research assessing the percentage of women's college graduates going on for doctorates in medicine and other fields reveals that it is not just the graduates of the most prestigious of women's colleges who achieve higher levels of distinction than their coeducational counterparts, while Bernice Sandler's research suggests at best a chilly, and indeed, in some cases, a downright cold, climate in many coeducational laboratories and professoriates. Sandler reinforces what we know from our scars in two-sex institutions: that equal access to colleges and universities has little to do with equal treatment. Women's colleges, founded to provide women with an equivalent to the education available to male students, still provide the best respite from a sexist society during a period of discovery and growth, enabling young women students to live self-confidently in the world of sexual discrimination to which they will return upon graduation.[2]

If these are the truths on which women's colleges have staked their right to existence, what are the current trends in higher education and our world which might give clues to the future? A trend in the last fifteen years of which we are very well aware is the much wider age span of persons attending college. The decline in college and university enrollment has been staved off chiefly by the influx of older students, the majority of whom are women. Our knowledge of lifelong learning, of continuing education, and of the importance of preparing for frequent changes of profession and work has contributed to a different concept of education's timing and purpose and has affected women's colleges significantly. This is not the first era in which older women have enrolled in significant numbers in women's colleges. Barbara Solomon has pointed out that at Radcliffe

[2] M. Elizabeth Tidball and Vera Kistiakowsky, "Baccalaureate Origins of American Scientists and Scholars," *Science* 193 (1976): 646–52; M. Elizabeth Tidball, "Women's Colleges and Women Achievers Revisited," *Signs* 5 (1980): 504–17.

from 1890 to 1910 the average age of students was twenty-nine. By the late 1920s, however, the average had dropped to between twenty-one and twenty-two.[3]

Women's colleges have used their experience and their ability to concentrate on the specific characteristics of women's lives in meeting the educational needs of women beyond the traditional college-age students. Recognizing the need for emotional and financial support in addition to access to education, women's colleges have made significant commitments to the older age-group: in the Sophia Smith Scholars program at Smith College, the Frances Perkins program at Mount Holyoke, or the Return to College program at Agnes Scott.

Another trend which has had a great impact on women's education and women's colleges is the many wider opportunities for women. We know of the dramatic rise in the numbers of women lawyers, physicians, and managers, and we are aware that women of all levels of educational achievement have entered the work force. It is now the norm for mothers to be in the paid labor force rather than to be at home with children. Because of continuing economic pressures, this trend is not likely to be reversed, and women of all ages will be preparing for a wide variety of careers through education in the liberal arts or by specifically professional training, such as for teaching. With the current attention by governors, commissions, and the public, teaching once again stands to be a respected profession for women and men. Certainly Mount Holyoke College had an enviable record of sending forth teachers as the vision of Mary Lyon was translated into graduates from those college halls.

Patricia Palmieri writes that "the fitness of women for higher education was a controversial topic in the nineteenth century; at issue today is the fitness of education for women."[4] Wom-

[3] Barbara Solomon, *In the Company of Educated Women* (New Haven: Yale University Press, 1985): 70.
[4] Patricia Palmieri, "The Matter of Difference: The Women's College Tradition in Higher Education," unpublished essay.

en's colleges have always addressed the issue of curricula suited
to women. President M. Carey Thomas of Bryn Mawr sought
to teach women the "men's curriculum," which denoted seriousness of purpose and equal access to classical learning and
scholarship for women of her era. But in the last fifteen or
twenty years we have finally learned what, with the same seriousness of purpose and undergirded by research in the liberal
arts, a true women's curriculum might be. The redesign of
liberal arts curricula to reflect women's experiences, as well as
men's, has depended in large part on the research on women
and special courses in women's studies in the *universities* of
this country, but it has been possible for women's colleges to
do more holistic curriculum change, to take seriously the
implications of the research on women, insisting that the basic
courses and syllabi take into account that women are more
than half the human race and that our stories and our perspective are as valuable as those of the dominant sex in our culture.

Another trend of fundamental importance is the growth of
an interdependent global community in which women's concerns often reflect fundamental economic, social, and political realities. One of the crucial strengths of women's colleges,
the provision of an affirming climate for women's development as intellectuals and leaders, sometimes has kept women
faculty and young women students from recognizing the need
for a feminist critique of society. The graduates of women's
colleges have been and continue to be self-confident women,
but they may see themselves able to achieve as individuals
without having come to grips with a world which discriminates
against women, even against women as well prepared and self-
confident as they are. Women's colleges generally have given
women a better chance of living full lives in a male-dominated
world, but although their very founding was a response to discriminatory practices in education, too seldom have they articulated a feminist critique which would enable its graduates to
go beyond individualistic responses to a discriminatory world.
Where this step is taken, the analysis of women's situation

quickly expands beyond attention to those women who have access to higher education and raises questions about other women and other groups.

In my work as an educator, I am most proud of the Balanced Curriculum project which I initiated at Wheaton College, for its effect both on that institution and, through others who have brought the project to fruition, on higher education in general. The second summer conference of that project at Wheaton in 1985 emphasized reaching beyond the white middle class. From a realization of the narrowness of our curricula has also come greater emphasis on the breadth of human perspective, an inclusion of those who have traditionally been powerless, the "outsider." Women's studies have opened our eyes to working-class women, women of color, and women of other cultures.

Certainly the tenor of the United Nations Conference on Women in Nairobi should have sensitized all observers to the fundamental questions facing women in most of the world. Sanitation, food production, health concerns, and human rights are basic issues of *survival* for untold millions of women, and our actions in consumer nations affect our sisters overseas. Cash crops grown in developing nations to feed Europeans and Americans deprive rural citizens in West Africa of the possibility of adequate nutrition. Manufacturing of chemicals by international corporations endangers the lives of citizens of any nationality where their plants are placed, and economic collapse in Latin American countries affects the banks of the United States and Europe to a significant degree.

Whether within the borders of the United States or outside, our cultural perspectives must be widened to include all women. We must cooperate more closely with women's groups and colleges around the world, increasing our understanding of the issues affecting our sisters in both the less and the more developed parts of the world. We can learn from both. I have little sympathy with an alumna of my institution, formerly on the staff of the Reagan White House, who wrote to the *Atlanta Constitution* criticizing the very idea of the United Nations Conference on Women in Nairobi held in 1985. She asked: Do men and women not care about the same issues? Of course, persons of both sexes care about justice, development, and peace. But for anyone to be unaware that these issues are experienced differently by women and men is no longer excusable. Consider the woman in Burkina Faso who begins her day at 4:30 A.M. while her husband is sleeping, who treks to the water supply, returns to prepare a meager breakfast if she is fortunate to have anything to prepare at all, feeds her husband and children, works in the fields and gardens all day long, cooks, and does the household chores of the evening; she sleeps about five hours while her husband has the luxury of eight. These are the realities of which women in our colleges must become aware. We, along with our sisters and brothers in coeducational institutions, must broaden our vision while continuing to affirm the worthiness of women. Taking into account that our world does not really believe in the worthiness of women, we must work to make this world a place of fulfillment for all our sisters.

The methods available to accomplish this task are varied and largely familiar to academics everywhere. The most effective is undoubtedly some experience for each student of a culture quite different from her own. Students who have witnessed the conditions under which millions live in India or Mexico or Bangladesh will never view their own lives and culture in the same way, for these are life-changing experiences. Interaction with international students and professors on campus is another method, but it is effective only if the exchange of cultural knowledge goes in both directions: American students learning about others' cultures as well as international students learning to cope with and understand life in the United States. The opportunities for curricular application of a global perspective are legion, from foreign-language study to anthropology to political science for international and transnational business, to ecology, to issues of conflict resolution and peacemaking. None of these methods is unique to women's colleges, of course; but the ability to focus on women around the world does change the nature of the cross-cultural experience, and this is a significant way of contrasting all aspects of the two cultures.

In order to pursue the important tasks which women's colleges have before them, it will be necessary to convince a greater portion of potential students (and their parents, in the case of the younger students) that women's colleges are the best places for women to be educated in the twentieth and twenty-first centuries, that until there is full equality of opportunity, not just for access but for advancement and for satisfaction in the workplace, there will be a need for a special place for women where they are the sole raisons d'être. We still have a great deal of ambivalence about this important principle; it is hard for us to say this institution is for women without adding, "But, of course, we have men involved in it as well." As Helen Horowitz has shown, the thread of fear that women would be unsuited for marriage by education and by the artificial single sex environment runs through the history of women's colleges.[5] The lesbian label has been used in both the nineteenth and twentieth centuries as a way to keep control of women's institutions and to denigrate sisterhood. The ambivalence so often observed in women's colleges between open proclamation of their existence by and for women and their desire for acceptance as normal must be resolved by society's becoming as readily accepting of women's potential as women's colleges are designed to be.

I do not agree for one moment with Barbara Solomon's statement in her history of women's education that "for present and future students the debate over the advantages of the

[5] Helen Horowitz, *Alma Mater* (New York: Knopf, 1984).

separate college environment is largely anachronistic," for women's colleges have considerable evidence on their side that they are the places where "women are always taken as seriously as men," a condition which Solomon desires for coeducational environments.[6] Indeed, Solomon's whole book is testimony to precisely why women's colleges are so essential. It would be disastrous for women's advancement to treat as an anachronism an institution which is the best hope for a woman-affirming environment in which women can acquire the confidence, understanding, and skills which enable them to flourish in world that still denies them their full due.

[6] Solomon, *In the Company*: 208.

INDEX

Index

Index

Index

Index

Index

Index

Index

Index

Index